Waterworks distribution, a practical guide to the laying out of systems of distributing mains for the supply of water to cities and towns - Primary Source Edition

John Ambrose McPherson

WATERWORKS DISTRIBUTION

WATERWORKS DISTRIBUTION

A PRACTICAL GUIDE

TO THE

LAYING OUT OF SYSTEMS OF DISTRIBUTING MAINS

FOR THE

SUPPLY OF WATER TO CITIES AND TOWNS

BY

J. A. McPHERSON, A.M. Inst. C.E.

Illustrated by 19 full-page Diagrams and 103 other Illustrations in the text, together with a Large Chart of an Example District, showing Distribution.

LONDON

B. T. BATSFORD, 94 HIGH HOLBORN

1900

Printed at THE DARIEN PRESS, Edinburgh.

PREFACE.

THE Author, having had upwards of twenty-four years' experience in Waterworks Distribution, feels confident that this short treatise will be of service to those interested in laying out systems of distributing mains, as well as to students and candidates for the Municipal and County Engineers', and other examinations.

He desires to acknowledge his indebtedness to the Council of the Institution of Civil Engineers, and to those engineers and manufacturers who have sanctioned the reproduction of many of the illustrations appearing in this publication. He would also tender his best thanks to those gentlemen who have permitted reference to the rules and formulæ employed by them, and who have in various other ways aided him in the preparation of this work.

J. A. M^cP.

July 1900.

CONTENTS.

DISTRIBUTING SYSTEM.

CHAPTER I.

GENERAL ARRANGEMENT OF SUPPLY TO DISTRICT OF DISTRIBUTION.

CHAPTER II.

NOTES UPON SYSTEM OF DISTRIBUTION.

CHAPTER III.

DETAILS OF METHOD OF LAYING OUT DISTRIBUTING MAINS.

CHAPTER IV.

PIPES AND FITTINGS UPON DISTRIBUTING SYSTEM

CHAPTER V.

METERS AND MEASUREMENT OF WATER, AND REGULATING AND RECORDING APPARATUS.

LIST OF DIAGRAMS.

LIST OF TEXT ILLUSTRATIONS.

INTRODUCTORY REMARKS UPON THE SOURCES OF SUPPLY AND STORAGE OF WATER.

BEFORE proceeding to the details of distribution, it will be well to notice briefly the sources of supply and storage of water, and method of delivery to the town or district to be served.

Broadly speaking, the supply may be either by gravitation or pumping, or from mixed sources.

Gravitation Supplies must be obtained from sources at sufficient altitude to permit of a natural flow to the towns or districts to be served. Such supplies may be obtained from copious springs breaking forth on the spurs of hilly ranges, and may be taken at the points where they issue, and be carried thence by pipe lines under their natural head direct to the town mains or to service reservoirs adjacent to the district to be supplied. Such sources can very rarely be employed without provision being made for storage, to equalise the flow and provide a reserve for dry times, as well as to furnish compensation water to the mill-owners and others having water rights in the districts where the springs are acquired.

Gravitation sources are more often, especially for large waterworks undertakings, derived from the catchment or drainage area of upland districts, and the water must be impounded in artificial lakes or storage reservoirs, unless the waters from natural lakes can be utilised.

Pumping Supplies may be derived from deep wells, or bore-holes, or from rivers, and it is also generally necessary with such sources of supply to provide storage reservoirs as a reserve to draw upon in dry times.

Mixed Sources of Supply are resorted to in many instances, the pumping sources serving to supplement the gravitation supplies.

Regarding the respective merits of the various sources of supply, much is to be said in favour of gravitation sources from upland districts, as they are generally very pure waters and the cost of pumping is dispensed with, although the capital outlay is generally much greater than with pumping sources, owing to the large cost of impounding reservoirs and great lengths of aqueduct, such sources being generally obtained from a considerable distance.

The quality of the water from deep wells or bore-holes is generally very good. Perhaps the least desirable supplies are those obtained from rivers in lowland districts, although when filtered they often prove satisfactory, a notable instance being the supplies obtained from the Thames for the Metropolis.

WATERWORKS DISTRIBUTION.

CHAPTER I.

GENERAL ARRANGEMENT OF SUPPLY TO DISTRICT OF DISTRIBUTION.

THE water for the supply of a town, from whatever sources derived, is usually delivered into one or more service reservoirs adjacent to the districts to be served. Such reservoir or reservoirs are generally designed to hold not less than three days' supply of water, as a safeguard against accident or temporary derangement of the pumping system, or lines of pipes or aqueduct.

If the service reservoir into which the gravitation or pumping sources are delivered is situated at the necessary altitude to supply the whole system of distribution, with water under sufficient statical head to ensure a good working pressure at all points, we have a town supply in its simplest form, and all that remains to be done is to lay off the distributing mains ; but it seldom happens that one zone of pressures will suffice, on account of the diversity of levels in the district to be served with water, and it becomes necessary to divide the district up under two or more zones of pressure.

When such is the case, the supply is first delivered into the service reservoir, holding three days' supply as

A

before described. This may be termed the "low-level" or "low-service" reservoir, and from it will be served that portion of the system of distribution that is situated at the lower levels, where the low-service reservoir will give sufficient statical head for a satisfactory pressure in the distributing pipes, and the district supplied under this zone will be termed the "low-level" or "low-service" district.

In order to deal with the high-level portion of the district, a district pumping station, or what is generally termed a high-level pumping station, has to be introduced. This is usually situated close to the low-service reservoir, from whence the pumping engines draw their supply, which they pump to the summit of the high-service district into a high-level water-tower, or over a stand-pipe.

A stand-pipe is generally arranged in conjunction with a high-service reservoir or tank. The water pumped from the low-service reservoir is forced against the statical head due to the height of the stand-pipe, and the supplies for the higher portion of the high-level district are branched off the pumping main before it reaches the stand-pipe; such supplies having a statical head or pressure due to pumping against the height of the stand-pipe. The balance of the water that goes over the stand-pipe falls through the down leg and enters the high-service reservoir, from which it is conveyed by the leading mains for distribution to the lower portion of the high-service district.

Stand-pipes are also used in low-lying and flat districts, where no convenient point is obtainable at sufficient elevation for a low-service reservoir, in order that, by pumping against the stand-pipe, a statical head or pressure may be put on the distributing pipes branching out of the pumping mains, for the supply of the low-

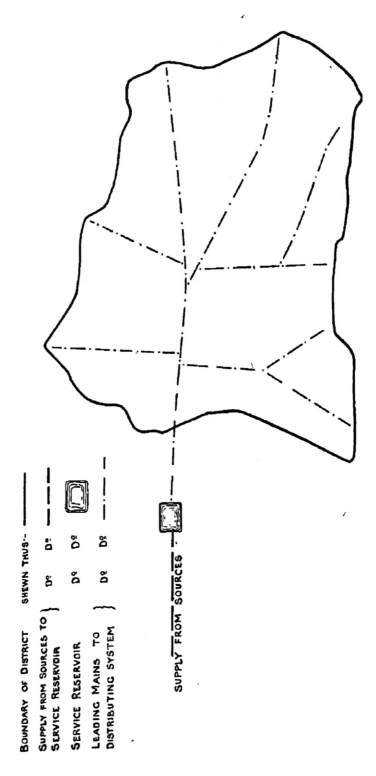

DIAGRAM No. 1.

BOUNDARY OF DISTRICT   SHEWN THUS:-

SUPPLY FROM SOURCES TO }   Dº   Dº
SERVICE RESERVOIR

SERVICE RESERVOIR   Dº   Dº

LEADING MAINS TO }   Dº   Dº
DISTRIBUTING SYSTEM

SUPPLY FROM SOURCES

level districts, in the same way as for the high-level zones described.

In any case, the purpose of the stand-pipe is the same, viz., to obtain what may perhaps be termed an artificial head on the distributing mains.

A high-level tower, although a costly structure, is very often employed, as it takes the place of the stand-pipe and high-service reservoir; but as the cost of construction of the tower, if of very large water capacity, would be excessive, its size is kept within moderate limits—about five or six hours' day supply being a reasonable capacity. It is pumped into from the low-service reservoir.

The five or six hours' capacity refers to a water-tower supply for a district containing a considerable population, as in the example in Chapter III. for the whole of the high-service district. But where the district is small, or only an isolated high-level zone containing but few inhabitants, as shown by Diagram No. 2, to be referred to shortly, a tank can be provided that will be of moderate size, to hold three-day supply; the limiting of the capacity of the tank to five or six hours is only where the supply for a longer period would necessitate an excessive expenditure for a very large water-tower.

The Diagrams Nos. 1 and 2 are illustrative of the types of town or district supplies before described.

Simplest Form of Supply.—An example of the simplest form of supply is shown in Diagram No. 1.

It will be seen that the service reservoir lies outside the district to be supplied, which is a necessary condition, as the range of levels in this case admit of the whole district being served under one zone of pressure from the service reservoir, consequently there is no point within the district where the reservoir could be situated at sufficient altitude to give the necessary statical head for a proper working pressure to the entire system of distribution.

The leading mains from the service reservoir are shown upon diagram, which is furnished with explanatory notes.

Compound District of Supply.—An example of what may be termed a compound district of supply is shown in Diagram No. 2.

It will be seen that the service reservoir, in this case known as the low-service reservoir, is situated in the high-service zone, at a point where it may be assumed the altitude is sufficient for the necessary statical head to serve the low-level district.

The leading mains from the low-service reservoir to the low-level distributing system are shown upon diagram

From the pumping station marked A, which adjoins the low-service reservoir, a pumping main is shown for the supply of a high-service tower, from whence the leading mains convey the supply to the high-level system

This diagram further illustrates what is a frequent occurrence, viz., smaller isolated districts at a high level, and the method of serving same by additional district pumping stations. These pumping stations obtain the water pumped to the respective high-level districts in the most convenient manner.

Pumping station B has an intake from the supply to the low-service reservoir, and an auxiliary supply off the leading mains to the low-service system of distribution, to serve as a stand-by in case of the supply main being turned off.

The second isolated high-level district is supplied

DIAGRAM No. 2.

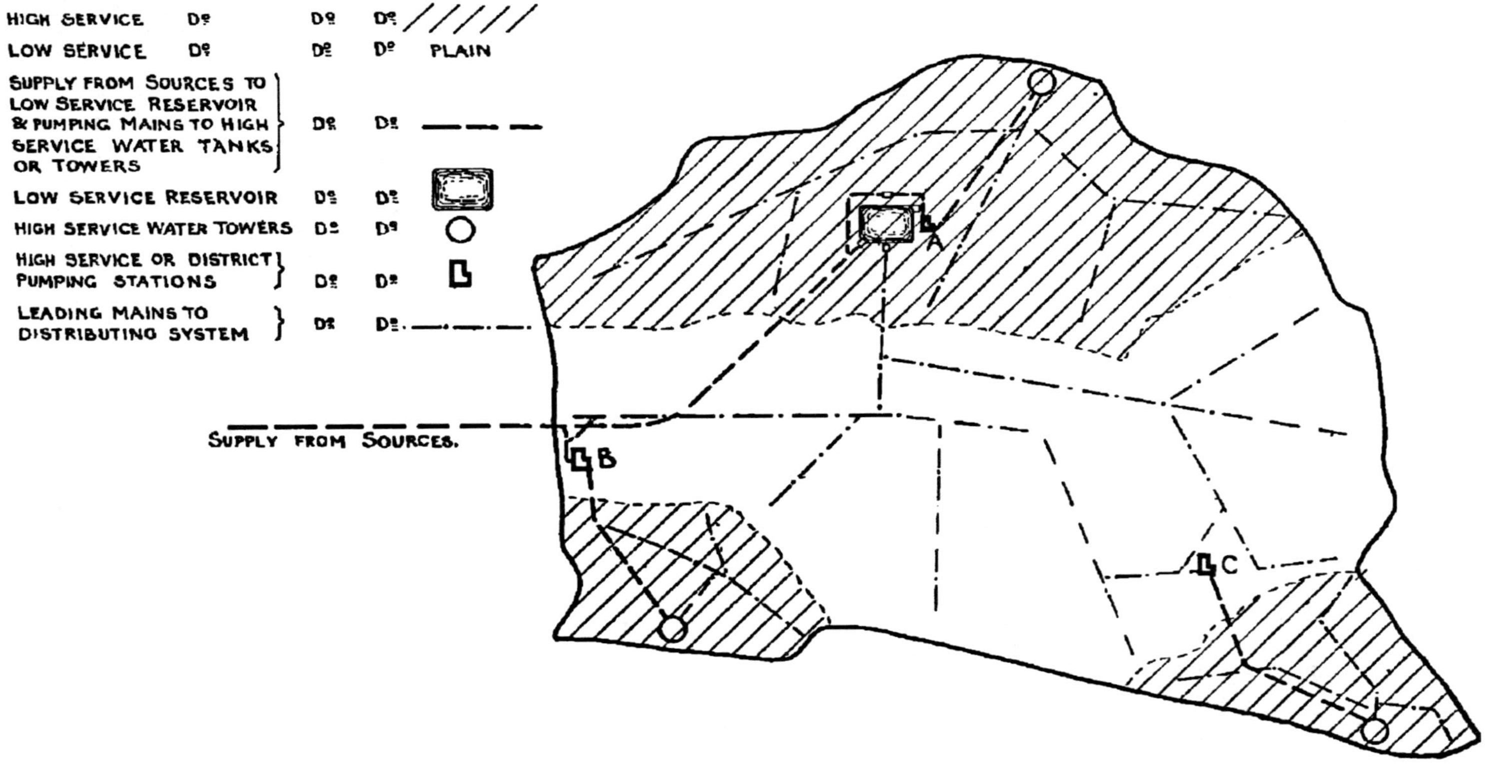

BOUNDARY OF DISTRICT, SHEWN THUS:- ————

HIGH SERVICE Dᵒ Dᵒ Dᵒ ////

LOW SERVICE Dᵒ Dᵒ Dᵒ PLAIN

SUPPLY FROM SOURCES TO
LOW SERVICE RESERVOIR
& PUMPING MAINS TO HIGH } Dᵒ Dᵒ — — —
SERVICE WATER TANKS
OR TOWERS

LOW SERVICE RESERVOIR Dᵒ Dᵒ ▭

HIGH SERVICE WATER TOWERS Dᵒ Dᵒ ◯

HIGH SERVICE OR DISTRICT } Dᵒ Dᵒ ⌐
PUMPING STATIONS

LEADING MAINS TO } Dᵒ Dᵒ —·—·—
DISTRIBUTING SYSTEM

SUPPLY FROM SOURCES. — · · — · · —

from pumping station C, the water pumped being obtained from the nearest low-service leading main.

In this instance there is no connection from the supply main to the low-service reservoir, on account of its being too remote; but a second supply is derived from another leading main, as a safeguard against failure. This diagram is also furnished with explanatory notes.

The two diagrams are good examples of simple and compound systems of supply, based upon the lines laid down in this chapter, and it will be apparent to the reader that the examples may be modified to suit a variety of requirements; but space will not permit of further types being shown, as it is desired to give the greatest prominence to the details of distribution.

Low-Service Reservoir and Pumping Station.— A general arrangement of the low-service reservoir and pumping station is shown in Diagram No. 3.

The main from the sources of supply enters at inlet tank A to serve reservoir, and the engines that pump to the high-level tower draw their water from reservoir at suction tank B.

A second suction tank C is provided, from which the engines draw their water at such times as the reservoir is emptied for cleaning or repairs.

A branch main D is connected to tank C from the supply main.

The delivery main to the low-service districts takes its supply from the reservoir at outlet tank E.

A branch main F connects the supply with the delivery main to low-service district for use when the reservoir is emptied.

The engine and boiler houses for pumping to high-level tower are shown, and the pumping main issuing from same.

Stand-pipe Supply.—Diagram No. 4 illustrates an arrangement of stand-pipe supply in plan and elevation. The stand-pipe is shown with the high-level reservoir adjoining. The head of water put upon the distributing mains, in the upper part of the high-service district, that are supplied off the pumping main, is that due to the height of the stand-pipe at A. The plan on diagram shows the general arrangement of the pipes. The supply for distribution off the pumping main under stand-pipe head is shown ; also the supplies to the lower portion of the high-service zone that come out of the high-service reservoir.

It will be seen that a branch pipe B connects one of the mains from the reservoir with the supply off the pumping main, the object of this being, that, in case of stoppage of pumping, the high-service reservoir will supply the stand-pipe district for what it is worth, of course with a much-reduced pressure, but sufficient to keep the distributing mains charged, and supply the ground floors of the houses (usually served under stand-pipe head) with water at a low pressure.

The stop-backs or reflux valves C and D reverse the supply in case of the pumping stopping as before mentioned, their action being as follows :—

When pumping over stand-pipe, the pumping head or pressure opens stop-back D for the passage of the water pumped to the district under stand-pipe head, and the pressure closes stop-valve C against the branch main B. Directly, however, that pumping stops, the water flows back from the reservoir through branch main B, opens stop-back C, closes stop-back D, and supplies the stand-pipe district from the reservoir as before described.

Before the modern requirements called for a constant supply under an ample pressure to reach the top of the

DIAGRAM No. 3.

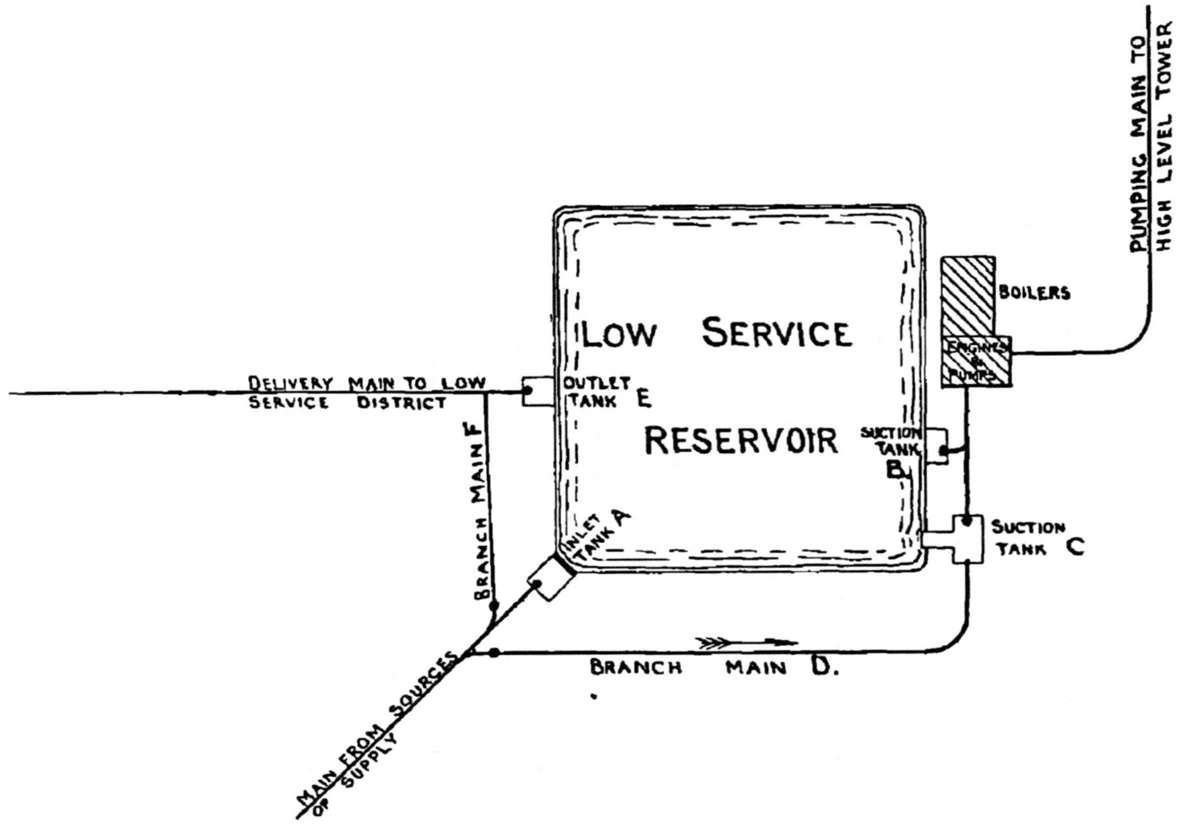

PUMPING MAIN TO HIGH LEVEL TOWER

BOILERS

ENGINES & PUMPS

SUCTION TANK C

SUCTION TANK B

LOW SERVICE

RESERVOIR

OUTLET TANK E

INLET TANK A

BRANCH MAIN D.

BRANCH MAIN F

MAIN FROM SUPPLY OF SOURCES

DELIVERY MAIN TO LOW SERVICE DISTRICT

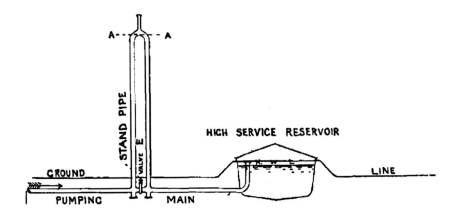

A----------A

STAND PIPE

VALVE E

HIGH SERVICE RESERVOIR

GROUND

PUMPING

MAIN

LINE

SECTION

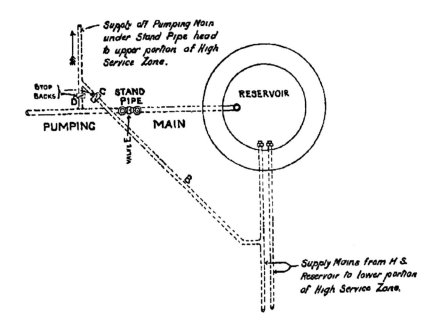

Supply off Pumping Main
under Stand Pipe head
to upper portion of High
Service Zone.

STOP
BACKS

D

C STAND
PIPE

RESERVOIR

PUMPING

MAIN

VALVE E

B

Supply Mains from H S.
Reservoir to lower portion
of High Service Zone.

PLAN

highest buildings for supply or in case of fire, it was only thought essential to pump under the stand-pipe head for a few hours a day. This necessitated the valve E being employed, which was kept closed whilst pumping under stand-pipe head, and during such period the upper portion of the high-level zone had the head due to the stand-pipe ; and reserve cisterns had to be provided at the top of the houses on this portion of the district, which filled during the time the pumping was thus under stand-pipe head. For the remainder of the twenty-four hours the valve E was left open, and the pumping was only under the head of the reservoir.

Now that a constant supply to all parts of the district is very properly looked upon as essential, it is necessary, wherever a stand-pipe system is employed, to pump continuously under the stand-pipe head for the requirements of the upper levels, and an intermittent supply should be deemed a thing of the past.

The author thought, however, that a reference to a method that has until recently been in vogue upon many water undertakings would not be out of place in the description of the stand-pipe system, especially as the valve E should still be fixed when erecting a stand-pipe installation, as it may have to be used occasionally for special purposes, such as alterations or repairs to the stand-pipe, which can be carried out by opening the said valve without having to stop pumping.

A by-pass and valve, shown by Fig. 1, which is perhaps a more convenient arrangement, may be substituted for the valve described.

The height of the stand-pipe depends upon the requirements as regards pressure.

Probably from 60 to 80 feet would be within the mark. If the former, it would represent a pressure at ground level at foot of stand-pipe of about 25 lbs. to the

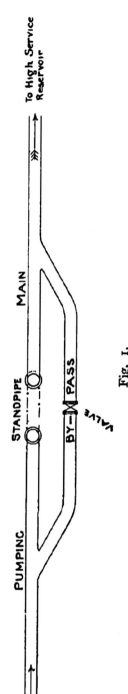

Fig. 1.

square inch, and if 80 feet high about 35 lbs. to the square inch.

And as the aim of the authorities would be to erect the stand-pipe upon the summit of the district, the statical head or pressure due to the height of stand-pipe would obtain at the highest parts, the pressures of course varying with the levels in the stand-pipe district, increasing to a maximum at the lowest points in the stand-pipe area of supply.

The upright pipe at the top of the stand-pipe is a provision for the escape of air.

Water-Tower Supply.—Diagram No. 5 illustrates an arrangement of water-tower supply.

The pressure of water in the district will be governed by the height of the water-tower, in the same way as with the stand-pipe supply before described, only that in the case of the water-tower system of supply it will take the place of both the stand-pipe and high-service reservoir. It is, in fact, a high-service tank, raised to such a height above the ground level by the supporting tower that it yields an adequate supply at the highest point of the district, and serves the whole of the high-level zone; and all of the leading mains for the high-level supply will issue from it,

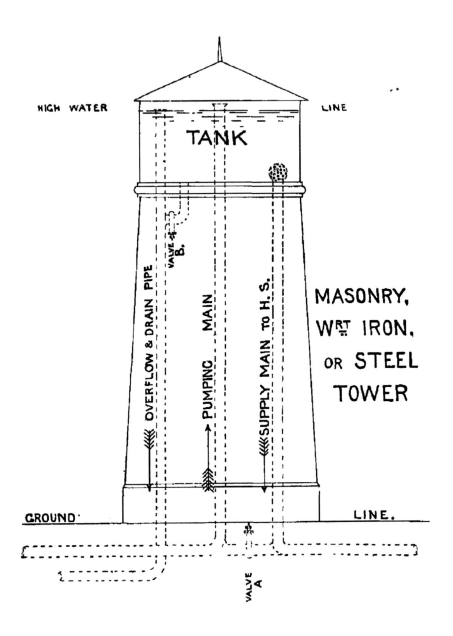

HIGH WATER

LINE

TANK

MASONRY,
WRT IRON,
OR STEEL
TOWER

OVERFLOW & DRAIN PIPE

VALVE B.

PUMPING MAIN

SUPPLY MAIN TO H.S.

GROUND

LINE.

VALVE A

B

unless in exceptional instances which will be referred to shortly.

Where money can be spent with freedom, the tower may be of a very handsome and monumental character.

A splendid example of a masonry water-tower is the Norton water-tower, constructed in connection with the Vyrnwy Works for the water supply of Liverpool (see Diagram No. 6).* It is 110 feet high. The supporting tower is constructed of New Red Sandstone, and has a very imposing appearance. The tank contains when full 650,000 gallons.

As a type of an iron superstructure for supporting tank, the water-tower constructed for the Shanghai Waterworks is a capital example (see Diagram No. 7).† It is of elegant design, octagonal in plan, constructed of eight sets of ornamental iron columns with radial and tie girders, and a central tube which acts as a stand-pipe if necessary. It is 103 feet high, and the tank contains 150,000 gallons.

I ought perhaps to say, as I have alluded to the Shanghai water-tower, that that particular one is not in connection with a high-level zone of supply, but is the low-service tank, as there is only one zone of supply in Shanghai—the whole district being on alluvial ground and very flat, and the nearest eminence sufficiently high for a service reservoir to command the district under a statical head necessary for an adequate pressure is twenty miles distant. It would be well, therefore, to remark, *en passant*, that with a water supply in its simplest form, viz., the whole district under one zone of supply, as before described and illustrated by Diagram No. 1, if

---

* Deacon on The Liverpool Waterworks, Minutes of Proceedings of Institution of Civil Engineers, vol. cxxvi.

† Hart on Shanghai Waterworks, Minutes of Proceedings of Institution of Civil Engineers, vol. c.

there is no spot within a reasonable distance at sufficient altitude, the water-tower may take the place of the ordinary service reservoir. This will be on all fours with the instances cited in the early part of this chapter of stand-pipes being used in low-lying and flat districts, where no spot is obtainable at sufficient elevation for a low-service reservoir.

Referring to the typical diagram, No 5, of the water-tower, the pumping main will be seen, also the supply main issuing from the tower. A connection or by-pass is made between these two mains at the foot of the tower, the object being that in case of having to clean or repair the tank, the supply main can be pumped direct into by opening valve A, and the vertical leg of the pumping main acts somewhat in the same way as a stand-pipe, only that the supply and distributing mains to the district are dead ends on the outlet side of the vertical pipe. The man at the pumping station regulates the speed of the engines by watching the pressure gauge, so as to keep a head or pressure on the pumping main which is just sufficient for the water pumped to rise to the top of the vertical pipe, thereby keeping up the same pressure or head on the high-level district as if it were being served as usual from the tower. Of course this is only a temporary expedient while the tank is emptied, as it is necessarily accompanied by a considerable waste of water, because it is impossible to pump to such a nicety as to just keep the district supplied and the vertical pipe full so as to maintain the head, without a good deal going over the top of the vertical pipe. In the same way, that with a stand-pipe supply, as before described, owing to the fluctuations of draught, to maintain the full stand-pipe head, a large margin of water must fall over the down leg of stand-pipe into the high-level reservoir But in this instance it falls over the open top of the

WATER-TOWER, VYRNWY WATERWORKS.

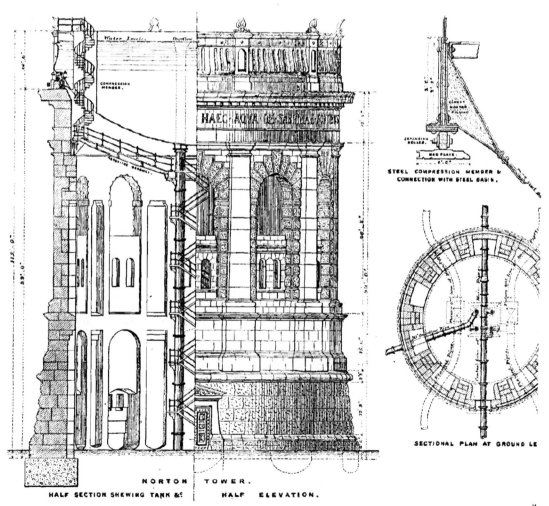

Water Level.   Overflow.

COMPRESSION MEMBER.

HAEC AQVA DE SABRINAE FONTE

STEEL COMPRESSION MEMBER &
CONNECTION WITH STEEL BASIN.

SECTIONAL PLAN AT GROUND LE

NORTON TOWER.

HALF SECTION SHEWING TANK &c   HALF ELEVATION.

WATER-TOWER, SHANGHAI WATERWORKS.

ELEVATION.

PLAN.

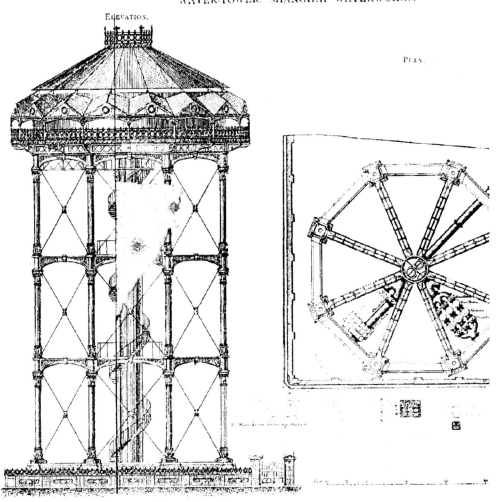

vertical leg of pumping main, and the valve B is opened to let such surplus water away through the overflow and drain pipe shown upon diagram. If the tank is emptied for cleaning purposes, this flush of water is useful for rinsing out, and, in any case, it is but a small waste for a short period.

Although it is preferable to lead off all supplies from the high-level water-tower, there may be instances where the pumping main has to be of great length to reach a small and straggling high-level zone, and a large proportion of the houses to be supplied may lie on the route of the pumping main, in which cases it would be an excessive expense to come so far back with a supply pipe from the high-level tower, and it is therefore preferable to branch the distributing pipes for supply from the pumping main *en route*. When this method is adopted, it necessitates a modification of the arrangement of the pumping main and supply pipes in connection with the high-level tower, as shown in Fig. 2. Where the pipes for distribution, lettered D, D, D, are seen to branch out of the pumping main, and when the pumping main approaches the high-level tower, it divides into two branches, the one in the centre of the tank corresponding with the vertical leg of the pumping main in Diagram No. 5, and delivering its water by an open end above the high-water line. When pumping is going on, the water will deliver through this pipe into the tank, and the pressure will close the stop-back or reflux valve C.

Upon the pumping being stopped, the water in tank will supply back through the other pipe which corresponds with the supply pipe on Diagram No 5, and takes its water through a strainer near the bottom of tank, the water supplied back during the cessation of pumping will open reflux valve C, and keep the pumping main and distributing pipes branching out of it charged under the

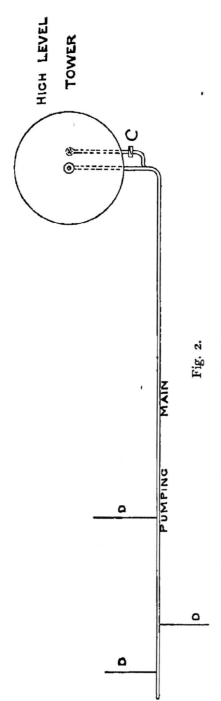

HIGH LEVEL TOWER

C

MAIN

PUMPING

Fig. 2.

head of the high-level tower until pumping recommences, when the pumping head to tower will close reflux valve and keep up supply in distributing pipes as before.

In the case of the tank having to be cleaned out or repaired under this system, pumping would be kept up as near as possible under the head of the high-level tower, the same as before described, and the surplus would flow away through the overflow and drain pipe as in the other instance.

The supplies for distribution in this case come off the pumping main, and will therefore be kept up by the pumping without any by-pass valve and connection as in the first instance, where the supply pipe was distinct from the pumping main.

In connection with a high-level tower supply, a middle course may sometimes be pursued.

The bulk of the district will be served by a supply pipe from the tower, separate and distinct from the pumping main; but it will

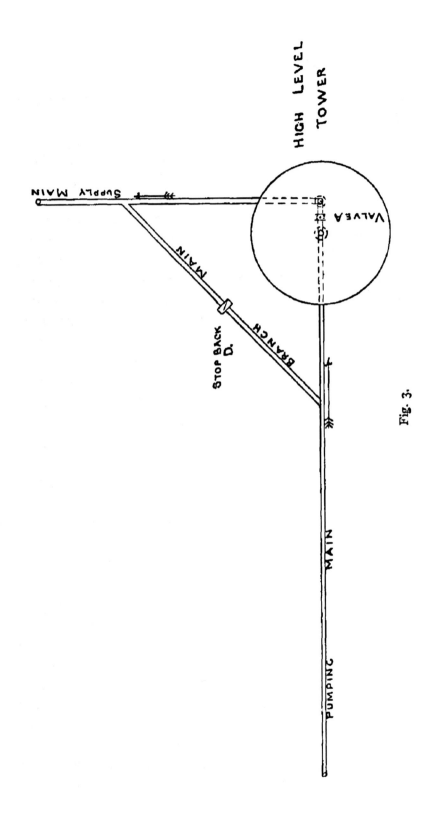

HIGH LEVEL TOWER

SUPPLY MAIN

VALVE A

MAIN

STOP BACK D.

BRANCH

PUMPING MAIN

Fig. 3.

be convenient to connect certain isolated supplies direct
to the pumping main, where they are remote from the bulk
of the district, and it would be an unnecessary expense to
carry distributing pipes back so far. In this case it will
be requisite to keep the pumping main charged back from
the high-level tower when pumping is not going on. Fig.
3 shows the general arrangement. There is a by-pass and
valve A to be used, as in the first example, to keep the
supply main charged at such times as the tank is emptied
for any purpose. But, in addition, there must be a branch
main and stop-back or reflux valve D provided to keep
the pumping main charged when pumping is not going
on, the action of which is as follows :—Pumping closes
the stop-back D, and water pumped goes direct into the
high-level tower in the usual way. As soon, however, as
the pumping ceases, the pumping main is charged back
from the supply main through the branch main, the stop-
back valve D opening under the head of water issuing
from the high-level tower.

The height of the water-tower will of course be that
necessary to yield a reasonable pressure in the highest
parts of the district, the particulars as to height given
in respect to the stand-pipe being applicable to the water-
tower, although, perhaps, one would be likely to allow
rather more margin in height in the case of the stand-
pipe than for the water-tower, as the former is in itself
less expensive, and generally intended only to serve the
highest parts of the high-level zone, whereas the high-
level tower is a much more costly structure, and has to
serve the whole of the high-level zone down to the lowest
level, taking the place as it does of the stand-pipe and
high-service reservoir.

Supply and Leading Mains.—The supply to a
town, when from gravitation sources, may be conveyed

DIAGRAM No. 8.

LINE OF AQUEDUCT.

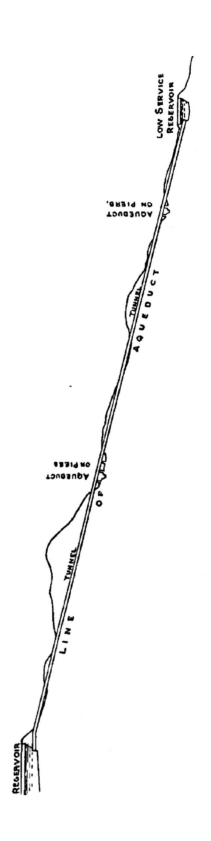

either by an aqueduct or by lines of pipes, according to circumstances.

An aqueduct can only be used throughout the entire route where there is a comparatively uniform gradient without any considerable depressions or undulations in the line of route, the primary distinction between the two modes of conveyance being, that with an aqueduct the water must flow under regular gradients, as in an open watercourse; while in a cast-iron or steel pipe line the water may flow under pressure, and the vertical section of the pipe line be irregular, as long as it does not rise above the mean hydraulic gradient.

The two modes of conveyance of the water may be combined in some instances; a line of aqueduct being employed for that portion of the route where a uniform gradient is obtainable, and pipe lines under pressure being inserted where considerable depressions or irregularities occur, or where it is necessary to dip under a river, etc.

Diagram No. 8 is an example section of a line of aqueduct conveying the water for the whole length of route.

Diagram No. 9 is an example of a pipe line all the way.

Diagram No. 10 is a combination of aqueduct and pipe lines.

A Line of Aqueduct all the Way.—Diagram No. 8 will be seen to follow the hydraulic gradient. The aqueduct is shown in tunnel for a portion of its length, and it crosses two short depressions on masonry piers.

That portion of the aqueduct which is in what is termed "cut and cover," viz., where it is laid partly in shallow trenches and partly by being banked over, will be constructed in masonry or brickwork or cement concrete. Where the tunnel occurs, the aqueduct will continue of the same internal section as before, and be constructed by completely lining the tunnel excavated, if in soft strata, with masonry or concrete or whatever material is used.

If the tunnelling is in hard and compact rock it will not require lining, except that the irregularities in the sides and bottom or invert will have to be rendered smooth by inserting concrete, as the flow of water will be very much retarded by friction, if the channel is rough.

Where the aqueduct crosses the depressions where streams occur, as shown upon section, it will be carried upon masonry or steel piers, and such portion of the aqueduct will be constructed of wrought iron or steel riveted tubes, preferably of the same internal section as the remainder of the aqueduct.

A Pipe Line all the Way (Diagram No. 9) will be seen to follow the natural section of the route, the only restriction being that it is not allowed to rise above the mean hydraulic gradient. Where a considerable elevation occurs, it is carried through a tunnel for the distance necessary to keep within the hydraulic gradient. The pipes dip under the beds of rivers, except in case of small and narrow channels, when it is more convenient to cross on piers. The pipe lines in this country are generally laid with cast-iron pipes, with spigots and sockets, lead-jointed. There is much to be said in favour of the cast-iron pipes. They are very lasting, the joints are easily made with lead, and the lead-jointing is elastic, which is a great advantage, as the joints give readily to any slight disturbance to which the pipes may be subjected by the settlement of the ground, or other possible earth movements.

DIAGRAM No. 9.

PIPE LINE.

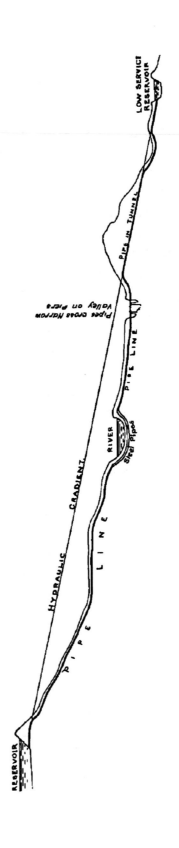

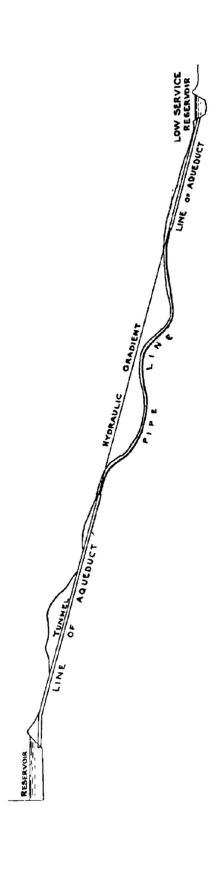

DIAGRAM No. 10.

AQUEDUCT AND PIPE LINE.

Moreover, when pipe-laying, the lead-socketed joints can, where necessary, be made to deviate slightly from a perfectly straight line, either horizontally or vertically, without having to employ special bends.   Where, however, a river or tidal estuary has to be crossed, it is very often found convenient to substitute steel tubes, as they are lighter than the cast-iron pipes, and can be bolted up together in considerable lengths, and conveyed on rafts or barges to the position where they have to be laid, and then sunk into the channel in the river bed prepared for them.   Also they have an advantage over the cast-iron pipes where they have to dip down and rise again at a considerable angle, as the lead-socketed joints, under such circumstances, are very apt to draw unless the sockets and spigots are held together by bolts and nuts passing through lugs on the spigot and socket ends; or unless the pipes are very well strutted, which is almost impossible in many cases where passing under waterways.

A Combination of Aqueduct and Pipe Line (Diagram No. 10) is very often employed, when part of the route where the gradients are favourable can be conveniently laid in aqueduct, the pipe line under pressure occupying the other portions of the route, in which valleys occur, and the levels dip considerably, or where crossing under river beds.

Very good examples of combinations of aqueduct and pipe line, upon a large scale, occur upon the Thirlmere Works for the water supply of Manchester, and the Vyrnwy Works for the water supply of Liverpool ; * also upon the new works in course of construction for

---

* See Minutes of Proceedings of the Institution of Civil Engineers, vol. cxxvi., and in *Engineering* for February 1889, November 1891, and June 1892.

bringing a supply of water to Birmingham from the Elan Valley.

Notes upon Hydraulic Gradient — As reference has been made to the hydraulic gradient, it should be explained that this term refers to the slope or gradient which governs the discharge of the pipe line, represented by a straight line drawn from the point where the head of water enters pipes, to the termination of the pipe line or point of discharge, as shown by Diagram No. 11.

Supposing the pipe line to commence at A, and terminate at B, the hydraulic gradient will be represented by the straight line drawn from A to B, having a fall of 1 in 100, and as the pipe line is below this line all the way, the discharge at B will be that resulting from a fall or slope of 1 in 100 for the size pipe employed. If, however, the pipe line rises above the hydraulic gradient A B, as shown by dotted pipe line which rises to point C, the hydraulic gradient A B will be broken, and the discharge for the whole length will be that due to the hydraulic gradient A C, at point C, which is a gradient or slope of 1 in 400. The discharge for the gradient of 1 in 400 will be but half of that for the gradient of 1 in 100, as by the hydraulic law " the discharge varies as the square root of the head."

When pipe lines have been laid down without due regard to the question of gradients, it has doubtless often led to very disappointing results and needless expense. For example, in the case illustrated, a 6-inch pipe laid within the hydraulic gradient of 1 in 100 would discharge .48 cubic foot per second. If, however, the hydraulic gradient of 1 in 100 were broken, and the pipe rose to point C, the hydraulic gradient of 1 in 400 would only give a discharge of one-half, as before stated, or .24 cubic foot per second, and the 6-inch diameter pipe from

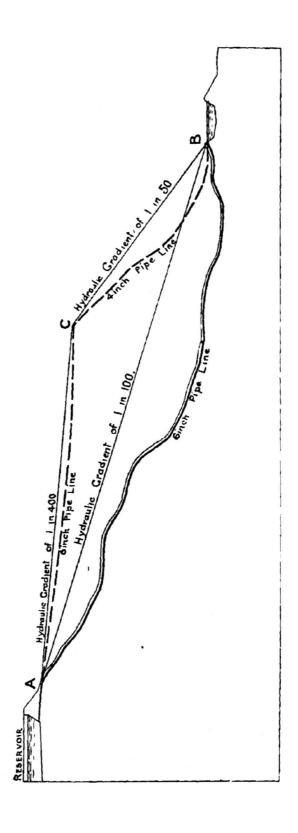

DIAGRAM No. 11.

c to b would be larger than necessary to discharge the .24 cubic foot per second on the steeper gradient for the remainder of the length.

Supposing the gradient to be 1 in 50 from c to b, as shown on diagram, it will be found that a 4-inch pipe is large enough on that portion of the length for the quantity named.

It will therefore be seen, wherever a pipe line rises above the mean hydraulic gradient, that not only is the discharge less, but if the pipe has been laid of the same diameter all the way, that portion on the steeper gradient is larger than necessary.

A section of the route of pipe line should always be plotted. It will then be apparent at a glance whether it is within the hydraulic gradient, and if the gradient is obliged to be broken, the size of the pipes can be properly apportioned to give the discharge.

CHAPTER II.

NOTES UPON SYSTEM OF DISTRIBUTION.

IN practice it is seldom found that a system of distributing mains is laid out with anything like scientific accuracy, because as a rule the pipes have been extended by degrees as the district to be supplied has developed, hence, unless great and almost prophetic foresight has been exercised from the initiation of the works, it is unlikely that the pipes will be properly apportioned as regards their sizes to the area and population of the districts to be supplied. In fact, when the pipes are first laid, it is generally impossible to foretell accurately the ultimate draught upon them.

It is, however, possible to estimate approximately the maximum population that will have to be supplied upon the various areas where the distributing systems are proposed to be laid out, bearing in mind the nature of the trade, or business, or residential supplies likely to be required in the various districts, which has a very important bearing upon the question of quantity, as will be pointed out in the course of this chapter.

The arteries or leading mains should always be of ample size for the probable maximum supply required.

There are indeed so many points that must be considered in laying out distributing systems that each case must, to a certain extent, be taken upon its own merits.

But it should be borne in mind that it is much

cheaper to lay a large-sized main, if there is any probability of increasing consumption, than to lay a smaller one and very soon have to duplicate it. For instance, a 10-inch diameter main will probably cost 25 per cent. less to provide and lay than two 7-inch mains, although it will have 35 per cent. greater carrying capacity.

Trade and Manufacturing Districts, and central portions of a city, where there are large and lofty shops and public buildings, require more main room than residential areas, as copious supplies are necessary for trade purposes, including hydraulic lifts and motors, large tanks for feeding boilers, breweries, laundries, aerated water manufacturers, private fire supplies, fire-sprinkler installations, and many other purposes, besides there being the necessity for immense volumes of water at the public fire-hydrants in case of extensive fires breaking out.

Residential Districts, however, require pipes of ample size, as they are liable to very heavy draughts for street and garden watering as well as the domestic supplies, and the population, especially in the suburbs, is constantly increasing, for which a margin must be allowed.

The residential districts vary very much in character, some parts being densely populated with small tenements closely packed together, where the draught is very heavy, while other portions have far fewer houses to a given area, yet in the latter case the residences will often be large and costly, requiring a very ample supply of water, and every provision in case of fire.

Between these two extremes come the ever-increasing middle-class suburbs of single or semi-detached villas, with their modern fittings, bath-rooms, and gardens, requiring an ample provision of water, so that all classes of residential districts should be provided with distri-

buting pipes of liberal area, well backed up by large-
sized leading mains.

Street Watering is a very heavy tax on distributing
mains, and should always be taken into account in laying
out a system of pipes, and the street-watering posts
should, wherever possible, be connected to the leading
mains, so as not to distress the system of distribution.

Levels.—In laying out a distributing system there
is also the very important question of levels. Although
a district may be divided up into different zones, there
must be a considerable range of levels in each, and it is
necessary to carefully consider these in planning out the
system. In those parts of the districts which are on a
comparative level, the more the mains are in circulation,
having regard to the avoidance of undue complication,
the better will be the supply; but where the levels vary
considerably, if it were not for the excessive cost, it
would be desirable to lay a separate set of leading mains
to each range of levels. This would, however, in many
cases necessitate the laying of great lengths of extra
mains, as a second lot of pipes would have to run through
many districts to reach the higher levels beyond. The
groups of distributing pipes to the varying levels should,
however, be kept as separate as possible; and leading
mains of large area maintained until the remote parts of
the districts are reached where those portions rise to the
higher levels. But when all the higher levels are adjacent
to the reservoir from which the leading mains issue, the
pipes should have a large area at starting, and until they
have passed through, and supplied the higher parts, they
should then be reduced in areas as they continue towards
the lower levels. By carefully arranging the sizes of the
pipes with regard to this question of levels, the evil of the

low-lying districts injuriously affecting the supply in the higher parts may be minimised.

As regards the laying out of the different zones of levels, a few general notes will be necessary, which will be supplemented by further particulars when we come to consider the details of distribution in the next chapter.

It has already been said that districts of supply vary greatly. Where there are no great range of levels one zone of supply will suffice, while in other districts the great diversity of levels will necessitate two or more zones of supply.

Statical Head or Pressure.—Broadly speaking, I am inclined to say that the maximum statical head need not, in fact it is better that it should not, exceed 200 feet. This is as great a head as the ordinary water pipes and fittings are generally designed for in regular working, although they are tested to a far higher pressure.

It is far better to have ample main areas, with the statical heads as herein recommended, than to have a very high statical head with restricted main room, because in the latter case, when the draught is heavy, it is likely to approach the full carrying capacity of the pipes, and the water will no longer be delivered at a satisfactory pressure, as the statical head or fall will be nearly all absorbed in overcoming the frictional resistance of the walls of the pipes. This point will be further considered in the next chapter.

In laying out a zone of supply, the head or pressure to be provided is a matter wherein some latitude must be allowed The very first consideration is an ample pressure in the most important districts. Fortunately for the laying out of town supplies, the principal parts of the town or central portions are generally comparatively low-lying, very often adjacent to a river or canal system.   Therefore if the maximum head is arranged at 200 feet, equal to 86 lbs. to the square inch, the central portions of the town will more often than not be within 50 feet of the lowest levels, so that there will not be less than 150 feet head, or 65 lbs. to the square inch, near the central parts.   But should the district continue to be thickly populated, and of an important character as it ascends to the higher levels, it will be well to reduce the range of levels in the low-service zone as much as possible.

The range of levels in the low-service district should in no case exceed 100 feet, which gives a minimum statical head of 100 feet, or 43 lbs. to the square inch, at the highest levels in the zone.

Where circumstances permit, it will be preferable to limit the range of levels to 80 feet, giving a minimum head of 120 feet, or 52 lbs. to the square inch.

In the example district illustrated by chart, and described in the next chapter, a range of levels of 100 feet for the low-level zone has been allowed, where the total range of levels in the district is assumed at 230 feet, because a smaller range of levels in the low-service district would necessitate a third zone of supply.

The high-level zone is generally in the suburbs or outskirts of the district, and more sparsely populated, especially in the higher portions.   Where such is the case, as exampled in the next chapter, a slightly greater range of levels may be allowed, especially if by so doing a third zone of supply is dispensed with.

In all cases, however, when laying out the system, it will be well to limit the ranges of levels in the various zones as much as possible, having regard to reasonable economy, as the less the range of levels in each zone the more satisfactory will be the supply.

Where, for instance, the levels range from 20 feet to

DIAGRAM No. 12.

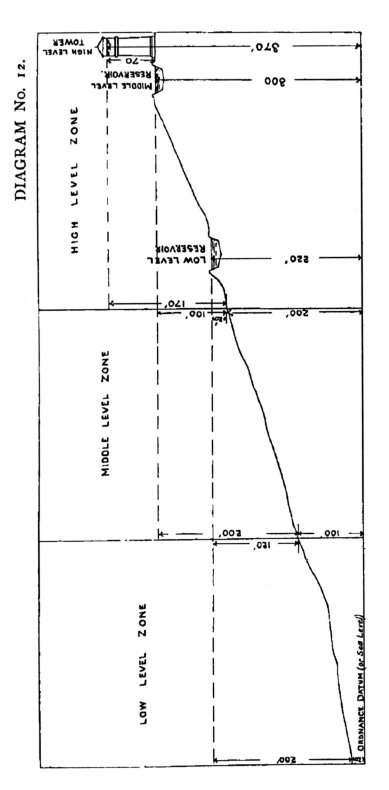

DIAGRAM of a DISTRICT DIVIDED into 3 ZONES

300 feet above sea-level, the district should be arranged in three zones, as shown by Diagram No. 12, which is a sectional diagram of such a district.

The low-level zone has a range of levels of 80 feet, and the middle and high-level zones 100 feet each. The low-service reservoir, or the reservoir for the low-level zone, is situated at 220 feet above sea-level, where it will give a maximum head of 200 feet and a minimum of 120 feet for the low-level zone; its position is shown in the high-level district 20 feet above the middle zone.

The reservoir for the middle zone is situated at the summit of the high-level zone 300 feet above sea-level, where it will give a maximum head of 200 feet and a minimum of 100 feet for the middle zone.

The high-level tower is shown at the highest point obtainable, its height being 70 feet, or 370 feet above sea-level, which will give a maximum head of 170 feet and a minimum head of 70 feet.

The high-service tower can be made of greater height, but the height given, and the heads for the several zones of supply, are laid out upon what are considered reasonable lines, having regard to the practical considerations touched upon, which must govern all such cases in actual practice.

Waste Water-Meter Areas.—Assuming that every modern water supply is provided with a waste-detecting system, it becomes necessary, in laying out the distributing mains, to so arrange them in groups that the whole district can be conveniently divided up into waste water-meter areas of suitable size, each governed by a waste water-meter. The author has had experience of the very great difficulty of applying a system of waste water-meters to the existing distributing mains.

Although it is desirable to lay all distributing mains from the service reservoir, rather than branch them out of the trunk mains coming into the district from the sources of supply, whether the supply be gravitation or by pumping, in order that the distributing system may not be affected by a burst on the trunk mains or temporary break-down at the pumping sources, yet there are instances where it is advisable to make exceptions to that rule. Where, for example, the gravitation or pumping main from the sources of supply passes through rural districts remote from the general system of distribution, and the company or corporation have powers, or are under obligations, to supply such district with water, it would obviously be an unnecessary expense to carry back distributing pipes, and in such cases the natural method is to lay branch pipes from the supply mains *en route*.

Positions and Depths of Mains.—A few notes upon the positions and depths of the mains in the streets and roads will not be out of place in this chapter.

The exact positions of the mains must be governed by the local circumstances, and as there are gas mains, and often telephone and telegraph pipes, besides electric cables, occurring in the streets, the rule of "first come, first served" applies. Generally speaking, however, the water and gas pipes are laid before the others, so that they have not to contend for position, except between themselves.

In all important thoroughfares where the roads are wide, and wherever tram-rails are laid, there should be a distributing main, or what is often termed a tapping main, on each side of the road, clear of the tramway, so that the service pipes can be laid on to the consumers on either side without having to cross the road and go under the tram-lines. A very suitable position for the distributing mains is about 3 feet from the edge of footpath. The gas-distributing pipes can be either farther out in the roadway, 3 feet distant from the water-pipes, as prescribed by Act of Parliament, or else in the footpaths.

Where the roads are not so wide, and no tram-lines occur, and generally in the residential roads, one distributing main will suffice, which can be laid about 3 feet outside of one footpath, and the gas-pipe on the other side of the road.

It is not desirable for either the gas or water mains to be laid in the foot pavements, unless the paths are wide and free from cellars coming near the surface. It is better that the telephone and telegraph pipes, or any electric cables for lighting or power, should be allotted to the footways, as they do not require to be laid so far below the surface for protection against frost as the water or gas pipes ; and this being so, they can be kept shallower in the footpaths than they could be laid in the roadways, as in the latter the heavy traffic, apart from the considerations of temperature, renders it necessary to lay all pipes at a considerable depth, so as not to be liable to breakage due to heavy loads passing over.

With the water pipes in the positions recommended, the fire-hydrants can branch into the channel course, in the best position for the water to drain away to the gratings when the mains are flushed or emptied for repairs. Also in such a position the mains, valves, and hydrants are easier of access for alterations or repairs than if farther out in the road in the full stream of traffic, or in the foot pavement. When in the latter, if the main has to be repaired, or if the covers of the surface boxes have to be moved to do anything to the hydrants, great inconvenience is caused to the foot

passengers, and if the water has to be let run the position is most unsuitable ; or in case of a fire breaking out,
it is a great drawback to have the fire-hydrant so near
the frontage of the premises, especially if alongside the
burning building.

The main-laying is also more conveniently carried
out, with less obstruction to traffic, where the pipes are
laid in the roadway, about 3 feet from the footpath, than
where the trench has to be excavated, either farther out
in the roadway or in the foot pavement.

Where, however, the roadway is in asphalt, or stone,
or wood setts upon cement concrete, it is well if it can
be arranged to lay the pipes in the footway, on the
score of economy, and also because, in case of a burst
main, the road surface, through being unyielding, does
not readily break up, and the result is that the water
finds a means of escape underground, and in many cases
a large quantity of the subsoil is washed away along
with immense volumes of water, into the nearest cellars,
causing great damage before the water can break out at
the surface of the road.   The first intimation in the
public thoroughfare of the burst is when the water has
washed out such a large cavity that the skin or shell of
concrete, with its surface-covering of paving, can no
longer sustain its own weight, and suddenly subsides
into the hole without any warning, perhaps carrying in
the footways with it, and seriously endangering the foot
passengers and vehicular traffic.   On the other hand, if
the main is under a non-retentive road material, the
water generally breaks out at once at the surface, giving
immediate warning of the burst ; and, moreover, as the
water has very little difficulty in reaching the surface from
which it can run away into the street gullies, it is far less
likely to find its way underground to adjacent cellars,
and the consequent damage to property is not incurred.

It is also much more troublesome and expensive to lay services from the distributing mains where the ground has to be opened in wood or stone paving on cement concrete.

In laying mains in roadways, all manholes or lamp-holes to sewers should be avoided, as a pipe where it partly rests on an unyielding mass of brickwork or masonry, and the remainder of its length is in a comparatively yielding subsoil, is liable to unequal strain, which frequently causes fracture.

As regards the depth at which the mains should be laid, the investigations which followed the severe frost in 1895 go to show that the depth from the surface of the roads to the top of the body of the pipes should in no case be less than 2 feet 6 inches, and in cold and exposed districts 3 feet.

The positions and arrangements of leading mains to the distributing system are governed to some extent by the requirements before mentioned, but the conditions are not in all respects similar. It is not of the same importance in what part of the road they are laid, as they are not tapped for consumers' services, nor have they fire-hydrants upon them as a rule. Where possible, however, steined roads should be chosen if there is a choice of routes, as the evils referred to in case of a burst, where laid under cement concrete, are intensified in the case of a large main on account of the greater volume of water. The depths of the leading mains should be the same as for the distributing pipes, not so much on account of protection against frost, as the strong flow of water precludes any likelihood of freezing, but a depth of 2 feet 6 inches is a safeguard against surface interference and surface influences where the ground is not of a solid nature.

There is an influence of temperature to which the

D

pipes are all subjected, other than the possibility of the water in them freezing, and which has probably been the most prolific cause of fracture of pipes in frosty weather, and that is the movement of the ground due first to contraction and then to expansion, as the moisture contained in the soil freezes; and lastly, to the loosening of the soil when the thaw takes place. The risk of accident to the pipes from these causes is minimised by laying them the depths stated.

In hot summer weather it is also an advantage to have the mains at a considerable depth, because the ground near the surface becomes heated, considerably affecting the temperature of the water in the pipes where laid shallow.

CHAPTER III.

DETAILS OF METHOD OF LAYING OUT DISTRIBUTING MAINS.

THIS chapter will be devoted to the practical details of the method of laying out a system of distributing mains for an example district as shown by illustrative chart.*

In laying out systems of distributing mains, the exact method of procedure must in every case be governed by the local conditions, and the probable increase of population. The general rules, however, as set forth in the preceding chapters, will hold good. We will proceed to consider a distributing system for a district as shown upon example chart, in which it is desired to provide for a population of 60,000.

It will be assumed that two-thirds of the population can be served from the low-service reservoir, and the remaining third from a high-level tower; or in other words, that 40,000 will be on the low-level, and 20,000 on the high-level zone.

In the first place, a low-service reservoir must be provided as mentioned in previous chapters, into which the incoming sources will be delivered. This reservoir to contain not less than three days' supply.

Taking the daily average consumption of water per head of population at 25 gallons, which is generally a sufficiently liberal allowance, where a strict supervision

---

* Placed at end of book for convenience of reference.

on the waste is exercised, the capacity of the low-service reservoir will require to be 4,500,000 gallons, arrived at thus :—

> 60,000 population × 25 gallons per head = 1,500,000 gallons.
> 1,500,000 gallons × 3 = 4,500,000 gallons for three days' supply.

Adjoining the low-service reservoir the district pumping station will be situated as shown, to pump to the high-level tower, for the supply of the high-level zone.

Duplicate engines* should be provided, each of which shall be capable of pumping in excess of the maximum high-service draught, so that there may be no failure in the supply in case of the high-level tower being emptied.

A fairly correct approximation of the maximum rate of draught may be taken at double the average consumption in twenty-four hours.

The maximum rate of draught in this instance will be .—25 gallons × 2 = a rate of 50 gallons per head.

This rate, applied to the population it is required to provide for in the example high-level zone, gives a little over 40,000 gallons an hour, or a maximum rate equal to 1,000,000 gallons per twenty-four hours. It will therefore be necessary to provide two engines, each capable of pumping at the rate of about 1,250,000 gallons in twenty-four hours, to give a margin in excess of the maximum rate of draught.

The pumping engine will work for as many hours, and at such times as necessary during the day and night, to keep a safe margin of water in the high-level tower, which should not be allowed to lower more than one-third to one-half of its contents during the hours of stoppage of pumping by night, and should be filled up

---

* The one to serve as a stand-by.

by the time the heavy draught comes on in the morning, and be kept full or nearly so by day, so that its full capacity may be in reserve in case of break-down.

For fixing upon the capacity of the high-level tower, it will be necessary to consider the average rate of consumption in the day-time. The draught is constantly varying, the maximum rate never being sustained for a continuous period of long duration, although it is likely to recur at any time between about 8 A.M. and 5 P.M., but on the average it is found that rather more than twice as much water is consumed between the hours of 6 A.M. and 6 P.M. than between 6 P.M. and 6 A.M.

The average consumption per twenty-four hours on the high-level zone at 25 gallons per head for a population of 20,000 will be 500,000 gallons, and dividing this quantity in the proportions stated, we arrive at, say, 340,000 gallons between 6 A.M. and 6 P.M., and 160,000 gallons between 6 P.M. and 6 A.M. The high-level tower should not contain less than five or six hours' day supply, or 150,000 gallons.

Proceeding now to the details of laying out a system of distributing mains for the district of supply thus briefly sketched. Upon referring to the illustrative chart of the example district, the high and low level zones will be seen, also the supply main and the low-service reservoir, and the high-level tower and pumping main to the latter, the general arrangements being in accordance with the previous diagrams. It would complicate the chart, and create confusion, to attempt to depict the dwelling-houses, business premises, or public buildings, especially as the width of the roads must be exaggerated to show the distributing system with any degree of clearness. In order, therefore, to indicate the business or manufacturing districts, that portion of the chart, where they are supposed to occur, is hatched with diagonal lines, and the residential parts left plain.

Density of Population.—The varying densities of population in a district to be supplied must be considered in laying out a system of distributing mains. For the example chart the area or acreage of the district of distribution relative to the population has had to be determined, and has been based upon the census tables, which give the acreage and population of the parishes and boroughs in the United Kingdom, the assumed population for our example being distributed over the area of distribution according to the best statistics obtainable, a certain rate of population being assigned to each class or district. The population in the business and manufacturing portions is made up of the permanent occupiers of the shops, and the numerous inhabitants of the side streets and courts interspersed throughout the districts, and abutting upon the principal thoroughfares. The densest populations are assigned to the residential districts immediately adjoining the central business and manufacturing districts, more especially, in our example, upon the north-east side, which is assumed to be the humbler and more crowded neighbourhood.

The population becomes more and more sparse the farther we get from the centre of the district of distribution, and the better class of residential suburbs are mostly apportioned to the high-level zone.

The Example Chart * is constructed to a scale for lengths of 8 inches to a mile, and is 24 inches by 16, giving an area of 6 square miles, or 3,840 acres. (Of course the scale is not applicable to the widths of the roads, as they have been exaggerated for the sake of clearness, as before mentioned.)

---

* Placed at end of book.

The total population spread over the whole area of the district gives a rate of population of about 15 to an acre.

The district is about equally divided in area between the low and high service zones, 40,000 population upon the low-level zone giving a rate of population of about 20 to an acre, and 20,000 upon the high-level zone being equal to about 10 to an acre.

The rate of population is naturally much heavier in the low-level zone, as it contains the densely crowded districts, and the business and manufacturing areas.

In the densely crowded districts the population is taken at 140 to an acre as a fair general estimate derived from the census and other tables

The business and manufacturing areas are estimated to contain about 70 population to an acre, due for the most part to the side streets and courts occurring in this class of district.

In the remainder of the district of supply the population thins out in the usual manner towards the limits of the district down to a rate of about 5 to an acre in the parts most remote from the central portion.

The distributing mains are separated into groups, the several groups being arranged in sub-districts, defined upon chart by dotted black lines enclosing such several areas or sub-districts.

Each group or sub-district contains approximately a population of 3,000, and the areas will be seen to vary according to the density of the population.

In the most densely populated part, where the population is estimated at 140 to the acre, the area of the sub-districts will be seen to be rather more than 2 square inches, as measured on chart, which is arrived at in the following manner :—

The chart is constructed to a scale of 8 inches to a mile, therefore 8 inches × 8 inches, or 64 square inches upon chart, represent a square mile; and as a square mile contains 640 square acres—$640 \div 64 = 10$ square acres for every square inch of chart, and as the densely crowded population is taken at 140 to an acre, 1 square inch of chart, equal to 10 square acres of district, will contain 140 population, multiplied by $10 = 1,400$ population; therefore 3,000 population, or the inhabitants of one sub-district, will occupy in the densely crowded neighbourhoods a space upon chart of a little over 2 square inches.

In like manner it will be evident that the area upon chart of a sub-district containing 3,000 population in the business and manufacturing parts will be twice that of the areas in the densely populated parts last mentioned, or rather more than 4 square inches, as the population is but half as dense, viz., 70 to the acre, or to express the figures in another form ·—

$\frac{1}{10}$ inch on chart $= 1$ acre, containing 70 population,
or 1 inch on chart $= 10$ acres, containing 700 population,
therefore 3,000 population $\div 700 = 4.28$ square inches upon chart.

As the population thins out the farther we go from the central portion of the district of supply, so the areas upon chart for the sub-districts become correspondingly larger.

The total number of sub-districts into which the whole area of supply in the example is divided is 20, of which 13 are upon the low-level zone, and 7 upon the high.

Grouping of the System into Sub-Districts.—The grouping of the system of distribution into sub-districts, each of about 3,000 population, enables the whole system to be conveniently controlled by waste water-meters.

The author has found that districts of about that population are a very workable size, and more easily inspected and kept under regular supervision than larger districts.

Some details will be given in another part of this chapter of the water-meter system and the methods of detecting waste. At present it is only referred to in order to explain the general arrangement of the distributing mains.

Levels.—Diagram No. 13 is a section showing the levels assumed for the example district, the levels for the low-level zone varying from 20 feet to 120 feet above sea-level. A greater range of levels in the low-service district would be undesirable, especially as the district is thickly populated up to the highest levels.

The lowest levels are assumed to be in the north-east portion of district, and the centre of the town is assumed to be about 40 feet above sea-level.

The low-service reservoir is situated at 220 feet above sea-level, thus giving a maximum head in the lowest levels of district of 200 feet, and 180 feet in the central parts of the town, reducing to 100 feet head at the highest levels in the low-service district.

The statical heads and corresponding pressures are tabulated below :—

	Head in feet	Lbs per square inch
Maximum at lowest level	200	87
Centre of town	180	78
Minimum at highest levels	100	43

A divisional line is shown upon chart at or about

a contour level of 120 feet above sea-level, between the high and low level zones.

The levels assumed upon the chart for the high-level zone range from 120 feet to 250 feet above sea-level. The lowest levels of necessity adjoin the low-level zone, and rise to a maximum of 250 feet in the south-west portion of district. The site for the high-level tower is of course chosen, where possible, on the summit of the district. It will be assumed that an elevated site has been obtained at 260 feet above sea-level, or 10 feet above the ground level of any dwelling-house in the high-level district. This gain in altitude, where procurable, for the site of the tower is a great advantage, as it reduces the height necessary for the tower, which means a considerable saving in expense.

We will assume the height of the tower to be 60 feet, which gives us an elevation of 260 feet + 60 feet = 320 feet above sea-level (see Diagram No. 13).

This yields a statical head of 70 feet in the highest part of the high-level zone, increasing to 200 feet at the lowest part, where the level is 120 feet above sea-level, on the boundary of the low-level zone.

It will be observed that a greater range of levels are allowed in the high-service district than in the low-level zone

This is because the upper portion of the high-level zone is very sparsely populated, only a very few houses occurring in the highest parts, whereas in the low-level zone some parts of the district are thickly populated up to the highest levels, and of course practical considerations override any hard and fast rule. It would be manifestly unnecessary to have a third zone of supply, or go to a very heavy expense in having a loftier water-tower than that named for a mere handful of houses in the highest parts. The range of heads

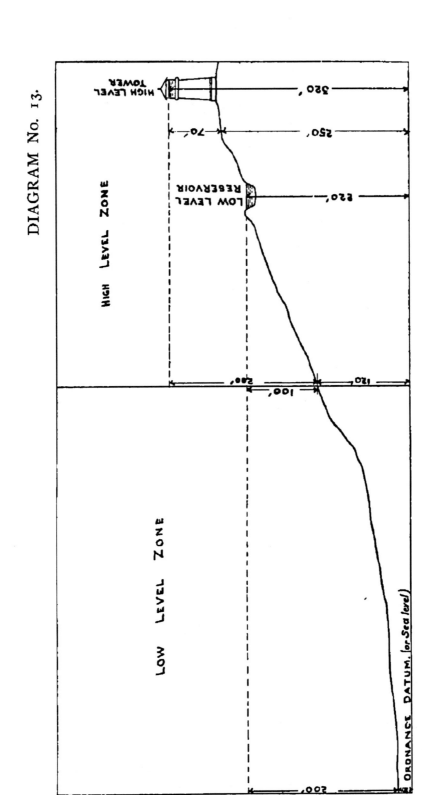

DIAGRAM No. 13.

HIGH LEVEL ZONE

LOW LEVEL ZONE

HIGH LEVEL TOWER

LOW LEVEL RESERVOIR

320'

250'

220'

70'

280'

100'

120'

200'

ORDNANCE DATUM. (or Sea level)

DIAGRAM of the DISTRICT shewn by CHART DIVIDED INTO TWO ZONES

and corresponding pressures may be summarised as follows :—

	Head in feet.	Lbs per square inch
Maximum at lowest levels -	200	87
Maximum at highest levels	70	30

General Explanation of Chart.—The population to be provided for in the example district has been already given in this chapter, also the capacities of the low-service reservoir and high-level tower, and the arrangement of low and high level zones, and the proportions of the populations in each zone.

The varying densities of population has been dealt with, and the levels of the districts and heads of water under which they are to be served.

We will now glance through the details of the system set forth upon the chart, after which we will take the low and high service systems in detail.

The main from the sources of supply will be seen entering the district in the north-west, and terminating at the low-service reservoir. The low-service reservoir and pumping station adjoining are shown, and the pumping main to the high-level tower. The supply main and pumping main are indicated by dotted blue lines.

The leading mains from the low-service reservoir to the low-level zone, also the leading mains from the high-level tower to the high-service district, are shown by dot and dash blue lines. The distributing mains in the sub-districts upon the low and high service zones are shown by full blue lines *

The sub-districts are numbered from 1 to 13 on the low-level zone, and 14 to 20 on the high-level. A thick dotted black line separates the low and high level zones, and the sub-districts are separated by thin dotted black lines.

The sizes of the leading mains are shown upon chart, but not the sizes of the distributing pipes. These are omitted from chart, except in one instance, for the sake of clearness. They will, however, be dealt with fully, and an enlargement of a typical sub-district will be given on a separate diagram, with the sizes of the distributing pipes and other particulars.

Formulæ for Discharge of Water in Mains.— Before proceeding further, it should be mentioned that the calculations for discharge of mains will be based upon Herr Kutter's formula, reduced into English measure by Mr Louis D'A. Jackson, C.E.

This formula gives results differing somewhat from the older formulæ, and it involves the coefficient of roughness of the internal surface of the walls of the pipes, which was not properly recognised in the older formulæ.

Herr Kutter's formula is now generally adopted in preference to others as giving more correct results. The broad difference between it and the older ones is that it gives smaller discharges for small diameters, and larger discharges for large diameters.

---

* The valves upon the distributing mains are shown by small solid blue circles, and the fire-hydrants where indicated by hollow blue circles, and the points where the mains diminish in size are shown by × marks.

Kutter's formula is, however, a complicated equation, and in its general form is, $v = c\sqrt{rs}$, in which—

$$c = \frac{41.6 + \dfrac{1.811}{n} + \dfrac{.00281}{s}}{1 + \left[\left(41.6 + \dfrac{.00281}{s}\right) \times \dfrac{n}{\sqrt{r}}\right]}$$

In this and the following formulæ :—

v = mean velocity in feet per second.
c = coefficient of mean velocity
s = fall of water surface (h), in any distance (l), divided by that
distance $= \dfrac{h}{l} =$ sine of slope
r = hydraulic mean depth = area of cross section of water
divided by wetted perimeter $= \dfrac{a}{p}$.
d = diameter of circular channel.
a = area of cross section of water.
p = wetted perimeter.
Q = discharge in cubic feet per second.
n = coefficient of roughness.

Messrs E. B. and G. M. Taylor, Civil Engineers, of 27 Great George Street, Westminster, have prepared an admirable series of water-pipe discharge diagrams in book form, based upon Kutter's formula,* which will be found very convenient by engineers, in order to avoid the perpetual repetition of calculations for the discharge of water mains Messrs Taylor found by experiment that the coefficient N for roughness, for uncoated pipes as ordinarily laid with the usual proportion of bends and undulations, was as nearly as possible .013, which has ·been adopted in obtaining the discharges for the purpose of this chapter.

The author has also found the hydraulic tables by Mr P. J. Flynn, Civil Engineer, which are also based

---

* Published by B. T. Batsford, 94 High Holborn.

upon Kutter's formula, of very great service, and can highly recommend them to those who require to obtain pipe and sewer discharges readily without having to go through fresh calculations on every occasion

Flynn's tables give the values of a and r, as well as the values of the factors $c\sqrt{r}$ and $ac\sqrt{r}$ for the various coefficients of roughness. Also the fall in feet per mile for various slopes, and $s = \dfrac{h}{l} = $ sine of slope, and the $\sqrt{s}$, so that the results can be readily obtained in whatever form required.

1. To find the velocity of discharge, we have the formula as first given—

$$v = c\sqrt{r\,s}$$
$$\text{or} \quad v = c\sqrt{r} \times \sqrt{s}$$

The values of $c\sqrt{r}$ for the given size and hydraulic mean depth are given in the tables agreeing with the coefficient of roughness to be adopted, also the value of $\sqrt{s}$ is given in the tables of slopes, so that the results are obtained with great facility.

2. To find the quantity discharged, we substitute the factor $ac\sqrt{r}$ for $c\sqrt{r}$, and have the formula—

$$Q = ac\sqrt{r} \times \sqrt{s}$$

The value of $ac\sqrt{r}$ is likewise given in the before-mentioned tables.

3. To find the diameter of the pipe required where the discharge and grade are given—

$$ac\sqrt{r} = \frac{Q}{\sqrt{s}}$$

4. To find the fall or slope required where the discharge and diameter are given—

$$\sqrt{s} = \frac{Q}{ac\sqrt{r}}$$

There are Jackson's and other admirable and exhaustive works upon hydraulics, which the student would do well to study, but as a ready means of arriving at accurate results, the diagrams and tables mentioned will be found of very great service. Much valuable information on the subject, and a large series of tables of velocity and discharge of pipes based upon Ganguillet and Kutter's formula, are given in Colonel Moore's excellent treatise upon "Sanitary Engineering" (published by B. T. Batsford).

DETAILS OF VELOCITY AND DISCHARGE OF WATER, AND SIZE PIPES REQUIRED FOR DISTRIBUTION.

Particulars of Leading Mains to the Districts of Distribution.—The leading mains for the low-level zone will be first considered.

The distance to the centre of the district from the low-service reservoir is approximately 2 miles, and the mean head under which the district is supplied about 150 feet.

The maximum rate of consumption has been stated at 50 gallons per head, giving for the population of 40,000 in the low-level zone a maximum draught in the day-time at the rate of 2,000,000 gallons per twenty-four hours, or 3.70 cubic feet a second.

By Kutter's formula in the abbreviated form given, to find the diameter of pipe required, we have :—

$$a\,c\,\sqrt{r} = \frac{Q}{\sqrt{s}}$$

Q = cubic feet per second, for 2,000,000 gallons rate per twenty-four hours = 3.70

$\sqrt{s}$ = square root of sine of slope, will be found by the table for a fall of 150 feet in 2 miles, or 1 in 70, to be .1195.

Therefore $a\,c\,\sqrt{r} = \dfrac{3.70}{.1195} = 31.$

And the value of the factor $a\,c\,\sqrt{r}$ nearest to 31 in the table, where n, or the coefficient of roughness, is taken at .013, will be found to be for a 12-inch diameter pipe.

E

It might appear, at the first glance, that the 12-inch diameter pipe, capable of discharging the maximum quantity required by the 40,000 population, would be sufficiently large ; but there are the considerations of trade, street-watering, etc., and an ample margin for fire purposes to be reckoned with, to which reference was made in the previous chapter. It is true that the maximum draught of the rate of 50 gallons per head takes these items largely into account. But supposing there were no contingencies likely to call for a greater quantity than would represent a maximum of 50 gallons per head of population, there would still be reasons why a larger main should be adopted, and these reasons are very apt to be overlooked when the size of the mains for distribution are being determined upon.

The required maximum rate of discharge of 2,000,000 gallons is the full carrying capacity of the 12-inch main, calculated upon the total available head of 150 feet ; hence to deliver that quantity the whole of the head or pressure would be expended.

In order, therefore, to provide for a reasonable terminal pressure at the points where the supply is delivered, there must be a considerable margin of main room, so that the available head may not be exhausted or reduced to an insignificant amount, when the demand upon the supply is at its maximum.

We must seek to ascertain what will be a fair and reasonable margin of main room, as it is quite clear that something larger than a 12-inch diameter main will have to be provided to give a satisfactory supply for the maximum draught, in the example being considered.

If instead of a 12-inch, a 15-inch main be adopted, comparing the respective velocities for a discharge of 2,000,000 gallons maximum rate per twenty-four hours :—

The velocity for the 12-inch pipe will be 4.73 feet per second.

     ,,   ,, 15 ,,   ,, 3.03 ,,   ,,

By a well-established empirical rule, a velocity of 3 feet a second is laid down as a suitable rate of flow for moderately large pipes. This would, in a measure, incline one to adopt the 15-inch diameter for the leading main where it issues from the reservoir, and until the first branch supplies are passed, providing that it is a size that will give a reasonable margin for terminal pressure at times of heavy draught.

Before proceeding to consider the last-named point, it will not be out of place, as the question of velocity has been referred to, to give a handy rule for obtaining the velocity for discharge, viz. :—

$$v = \frac{g}{2.04\ d^2}$$

Where v = velocity in feet per second.

g = gallons per minute.

d = diameter of pipe in inches.

Reverting to the question of the size of leading main. Assuming a 15-inch diameter pipe, what will be the head required to discharge the quantity of 2,000,000 rate per twenty-four hours, or 3.70 cubic feet per second?

By the abbreviated formula previously given in its fourth form, to find the fall or slope required :—

$$\sqrt{s} = \frac{Q}{a\ c\ \sqrt{r}}$$

The value for the factor $a\ c\ \sqrt{r}$ will be found by the tables to which reference has been made to be 61.867 for a 15-inch pipe. We shall therefore have :—

$$\sqrt{s} = \frac{3.70}{61.867} = .0598.$$

The nearest value in the table of slopes for .0598 will be found to be 1 in 279. This gradient for the length of 2 miles to the centre of the district will give a head of 38 feet, which will therefore be the head required for the maximum rate of discharge. As this is only 25 per cent., or one-fourth of the available head, it will leave a very fair margin of head to ensure the maximum supply being yielded at an adequate pressure.

The author will venture to adopt as a rule for determining the size of pipe for the distributing system, the margin as stated, viz., a main room that will yield the maximum rate of discharge with an expenditure of head in overcoming friction of 25 per cent. of the available statical head.

The writer has given a great deal of consideration to the question of main room, and believes that the rule adopted for the size of leading mains to the system of distribution will be found very satisfactory in actual practice.

It has doubtless been the custom in many cases to adopt the size (or one very little in excess of that) necessary to yield the maximum rate, and for this reason the supply has not been satisfactory, and has very soon had to be supplemented by auxiliary mains Also the distinction in apportioning the sizes between the leading mains for distribution and the supply mains is not always sufficiently recognised.

By supply mains are here meant the trunk mains bringing in the gravitation or pumping sources of supply to the low-service reservoirs, and the pumping mains to the high-level districts. If the maximum quantity these have to deliver is provided for as regards capacity of pipes, nothing more, or at any rate only a small margin of area is required to allow for obstruction by possible corrosion in the pipes, and so as to be on the right side ; because, as long as the full supply is delivered at the reservoirs, a margin of terminal pressure is not needed.

With the leading mains for distribution, however, the requirements are altogether different, as already explained; and a margin of area should always be allowed, so that the water is delivered in sufficient volume, and with an ample pressure.

If the whole of the supply to the low-level zone were conveyed to the centre of the district by the leading main, without any being drawn off *en route*, the pipe would be kept the full diameter of 15 inches all the way; and for the purpose of arriving at the size of main issuing from the low-level reservoir, it was necessary to base the calculation upon such an assumption. It will, however, be understood that as the sub-districts are reached by the leading main, when the points are passed where the mains branch off to the various distributing groups or sub-districts, the diameter of the leading main will be diminished from time to time, the branch mains, as it were, bearing their share of the area of main room according to the proportion of the total discharge which each leading branch conveys into the sub-district it serves.

The question of the extent to which the diameter of the leading main will be reduced as it passes the branches to the sub-districts will also be influenced by the considerations of the varying levels for the reasons set forth in the previous chapter.

Theoretically speaking, supposing the whole of the low-service district were at one level, and all of the sub-districts of similar character, the size of the leading main would be reduced after passing each sub-district by the proportion that each bears to the whole of the low-level supply, viz., by one-thirteenth.

But it is seldom if ever that a district is of uniform levels and character throughout; and in the example chart we have a diversity of levels and districts of varying character, the consideration of which will give the reader a good idea of what he may have to provide for in actual practice. In the example, the leading main has been diminished from 15-inch to 14-inch diameter, after passing the point at which the main to sub-district No. 1 branches out of it. This is a greater reduction in leading main area than the proportion which one sub-district bears to the whole low-level zone. But as No. 1 sub-district lies at a higher level than most of the low-level zone, it is desirable to reduce the carrying capacity of the leading main after passing it, in order to minimise the tendency that the lower-lying districts have of injuriously affecting the supply to the higher levels. It is better, therefore, in this case to reduce the area of the leading main rather too much than too little.

The size of the leading main has not again been reduced until after passing where the supplies to districts Nos. 2, 3, 4, 5, 6, 7, and 8 branch out, the reasons for this being that it is well to bring an ample-sized main into the heart of the district to the most important portions, and that districts Nos 4 and 5, which are very important, and run up to the higher levels of the low service, may draw upon as large a leading main area as possible.

We have by this time served eight out of the thirteen sub-districts, and as the maximum rate for the whole district is 3.70 cubic feet a second = to a rate of 2,000,000 gallons per twenty-four hours, the proportion for the eight sub-districts served will be eight-thirteenths (3.70) = 2.277 cubic feet per second, leaving a balance required for the remaining five sub-districts of 3.70 − 2.227 = 1.423.

By Kutter's formula, in the abbreviated form before employed, to find the diameter of the pipe required, we have :—

$$a\,c\,\sqrt{r} = \frac{Q}{\sqrt{s}}$$

Where $Q = 1.423$ cubic feet per second for the remaining five sub-districts, and $\sqrt{s}$ (taking the same grade as in the case of the 15-inch leading main) $= .0598$ Therefore—

$$a\,c\,\sqrt{r} = \frac{1.423}{.0598} = 23.8$$

And the value of the factor $a\,c\,\sqrt{r}$ nearest to 23.8 in the table before referred to will be found to be for an 11-inch pipe. A 12-inch main will, however, be adopted, as 11-inch is a size not usually employed; and, moreover, it will be well to keep a rather full area for the leading main, having regard to the importance of the central district, and until after passing the point where the leading main branches to the sub-districts Nos. 10 and 9, particularly as No. 9 sub-district runs up to the higher levels.

Directly, however, that the last-named junction is passed, it will be well to reduce the area of the leading main to the full amount proportionate to the districts served, as two of the remaining sub-districts, viz., Nos. 11 and 12, are low-lying, and would otherwise have too great a tendency to draw from the sub-districts passed, which are on higher levels.

As we have now served ten out of the thirteen sub-districts, a balance of main room is required of three-thirteenths of 3.70 cubic feet per second, or .854 cubic feet per second for the remaining three districts.

To find the diameter of leading main required for this quantity, we have :—

$$a\,c\,\sqrt{r} = \frac{Q}{\sqrt{s}}$$

Where $Q = .854$ cubic foot per second, and $\sqrt{s} = .0598$ as before. Therefore—

$$a\,c\,\sqrt{r} = \frac{.854}{.0598} = 14.28$$

And the value of the factor $a\,c\,\sqrt{r}$ nearest to 14.28 in the table will be found to be for a 9-inch pipe, which will be the size adopted to continue from the last-named point to where the main to the sub-district No. 13 branches off, and a 7-inch will run thence to the sub-districts Nos. 11 and 12. It will be unnecessary to prolong the calculations, as the particulars already given indicate fully the process of working out the necessary diameters for the leading main. We might call attention, however, to the size of the branch leading main to sub-districts Nos. 7 and 8, and to Nos. 11 and 12, being 7-inch in each case, which is rather less than the proportional size for the two sub-districts The reason for this is because they are low-lying sub-districts.

On the other hand, the branch leading main to sub-districts Nos. 9 and 10 is 8 inches in diameter at starting, and until it passes the branch to sub-district No. 10, when it diminishes to a 7-inch to serve sub-district No. 9; the larger area in this case is on account of its running up to the higher levels to supply No 9 sub-district.

Leading Mains for the High-Level Zone.—The high-level leading mains can be disposed of very shortly. It will be understood that the purpose of the chart is to serve as an example, in order to explain the principles and methods adopted in laying out the leading and distributing mains, and when this has been done it is no longer necessary to dwell upon the details set forth in chart. Having, therefore, fully considered the apportioning of the sizes of the leading mains for the low-level zones, it will be superfluous to go into the question of the high-level ones at any length ; they will, therefore, be discussed as briefly as possible.

The example high-level zone contains but half the

population of the low-level district, and the maximum rate of draught in the day-time will therefore be but a half, viz., 1,000,000 gallons rate per twenty-four hours, or 1.85 cubic feet per second.

To determine the size of leading main issuing from the high-level tower, the rule adopted for the low-level zone will be employed, namely, a main room that will yield the maximum rate of discharge with an expenditure of head in overcoming friction of 25 per cent. of the available statical head, and further, for the purpose of arriving at the size of the leading main at starting, it is necessary to pursue the same lines as with the low-level, assuming that the whole of the high-level supply has to be conveyed to a certain point or centre of district by a leading main the size of which is to be determined under the mean statical head available. Upon these broad lines it will be assumed from chart that the average distance to convey the water is about $1\frac{1}{2}$ miles, with a mean statical head of 140 feet, giving a fall or gradient of 1 in 56.

The size of leading main that will discharge the maximum quantity with an expenditure of 25 per cent of the available statical, viz, 35 feet fall, or about 1 in 225, will be found as before by the formula :—

$$ac\sqrt{r}=\frac{Q}{\sqrt{s}}$$

Where Q = 1.85 cubic feet per second, and $\sqrt{s}=0.666$ as given by tables for a fall of 1 in 225, which gives—

$$ac\sqrt{r}=\frac{1.85}{.0666}=27.8$$

And the value of the factor $ac\sqrt{r}$ nearest to 27.8 in the tables will be found to be between an 11 and a 12-inch pipe. The 12-inch diameter pipe will therefore be adopted.

The chart shows the leading main branching east and west soon after leaving the high-level tower. The total main room obtained as above will be split up in the proportions of supply upon the two leading branches. The supply running westward is for four sub-districts out of the seven sub-districts upon the high-level zone. This leading branch will therefore require to have a proportion of four-sevenths of the total main room, and the supply running eastward to the remaining three sub-districts will have the balance of main room of three-sevenths.

As the discharge is according to the value of the factor $a c \sqrt{r}$, we need not go further than to split up the factor given in the tables for the 12-inch diameter pipe adopted, which will be found to be 33.497, into the proportions of supply upon the two branch leading mains. Four-sevenths for the leading main running westward will be 19.141, and three-sevenths for the main running eastward will give 14.356. The nearest values in the tables for these two new factors will be found to be for a 10-inch main running westward, and a 9-inch running eastward.

The 10-inch leading main running westward will diminish to a 9-inch after passing the branch to No. 18 sub-district, and to 8-inch and 6-inch respectively after passing the branch mains to sub-districts Nos. 15 and 16

The 9-inch leading main running eastward will diminish to an 8-inch after passing the branch main to No. 14 sub-district, and to a 7-inch after passing the branch to No. 19 sub-district. The diminutions made in the diameter of the leading main running westward, after passing the several sub-districts, being the nearest proportional reductions that could be made, for the supply taken by each sub-district as the levels fall fairly regularly as the leading main continues through the districts, and it is therefore desirable to diminish its area in proportion to each district passed, in order to prevent the lower levels, which are reached last, unduly affecting the pressure in the higher parts

As regards the leading main running eastward, it will be noticed that the second reduction in diameter from 8-inch to 7-inch differs from the last reduction of 8-inch to 6-inch in the main running westward; this is on account of the very long length of leading main after passing the sub-district No. 19, before No. 20 sub-district is reached. When, however, that district is reached, the pipe supplying same is reduced to 6-inch diameter as the sub-district No. 20 is in the lower parts of the high-level zone, and as in other such cases the smaller sized branch to the distributing district is preferable, to check the tendency of the lower parts weakening the supply to the higher levels.

Particulars of Distributing Mains in the Distributing Groups or Sub-Districts.—Coming now to the question of the sizes of pipes required in the sub-districts. The thirteen districts in the low-level zone average a population each of 3,077, and the proportionate maximum rate of discharge to be provided for in each sub-district will be one-thirteenth of the total maximum rate of discharge, viz. :—

$\frac{1}{13}$ (2,000,000 gals. maximum rate per twenty-four hours)= 153,846 gals., or $\frac{1}{13}$ of 3.70 cubic feet per second =.28 cubic foot per second.

And by the formula for diameter of pipe required, viz. :—

$$a \, c \sqrt{r} = \frac{Q}{\sqrt{s}}$$

Where $Q = .28$ cubic foot per second, and $\sqrt{s} = .0598$ for the same grade as for the 15-inch leading main, we have—

$$a \, c \sqrt{r} = \frac{.28}{.0598} = 4.682.$$

The value of the factor $a c \sqrt{r}$ nearest to 4.682 in the table before referred to will be found to be for a 6-inch diameter pipe.

The minimum size for the leading branches to the sub-districts in the low-level zone will therefore be 6 inches ; but where the sub-districts reach the higher levels in the zone of supply, and in the most important central districts, the size of the leading branches to the sub-districts will be increased to 7 inches, and the sizes of the distributing pipes or tapping mains, as they are sometimes termed, in the sub-districts will be influenced by the conditions mentioned.

In the low-level zone, No. 1 sub-district will have a 7-inch leading branch, as the district is generally in the higher levels. Nos. 3, 4, 5, 6, 9, 10, and 13 will also have 7-inch leading branches, as they are generally in the most important central parts, and Nos. 4, 5, 9, and 13 run to the higher levels of the low-service zone.

On the other hand, the sub-districts Nos. 2, 7, 8, 11, and 12 will each have the minimum sized leading branch, viz., 6-inch diameter, as they are generally low-lying districts, and are not in the most important central parts.

In the high-level zone the size of the leading branches to the sub-districts will be regulated by the levels only, as all the high-level district is residential. Nos. 14 and 15 sub-districts, which are situated in the highest parts of the high-level zone, will have 7-inch leading branches, and the other five sub-districts, which are lower lying, will have 6-inch leading branches.

In order to illustrate clearly the arrangement of the distributing mains, an enlargement is shown by Diagram No. 14 of the sub-district numbered 5 on chart, which is a good example of a distributing group or sub-district in the central part of the district of supply.

The two most important considerations in connection

with the laying out of the sub-districts, after determining the sizes of the leading branch mains, are the arrangement of the distributing pipes and valves, and the sizes of the mains.

The author strongly advocates the system shown upon example chart, of putting the distributing pipes in circulation where practicable by supplying the mains in each section or division of the sub-districts from two directions.

The only disadvantages in this method are that the distributing mains are rather more complicated, and more turn-off valves are necessary, and the labour in turning off the various sections in the sub-districts is slightly greater.

The advantages, however, far more than compensate for the drawbacks mentioned. In the first place, the more complete the circulation, the less chance there is of complaints arising through dead or stagnant water, which may happen where there are a lot of separate main ends, especially in long straggling roads where there are but few supplies, and the draught is in consequence slight near the ends.

In the second place, the mains being connected both ways, doubles their capacity, which is a very great advantage at times of heavy draught.

It is obvious that wherever the mains in a particular section have to be drawn upon in case of fire, if they are supplied from two directions off mains well backed up, the fire-hydrants upon the said section will be served with double the quantity that would be available if the supply was coming from one direction only, and double the number of hydrants will be able to be drawn upon.

If we consider in detail the arrangement of the distributing pipes, and their sizes as shown by enlargement of sub-district No. 5, the method of laying out all the distributing groups or sub-districts in a district of supply will be understood to follow the same principles and details of further types of sub-districts will be unnecessary.

The several sections or divisions of the sub-district will be seen to have in all cases a supply from more than one direction, as before recommended, and the valves are so placed that each section is separately controlled.

The first necessity, as before explained, is the splitting up of the whole of the area of distribution into separate and distinct sub-districts, each of which will be a waste water-meter district. This necessitates a very careful and systematic arrangement of the mains. The waste water-meter system is therefore a great advantage, apart from the prevention of waste, on account of its calling for a very careful setting out of the distributing pipes.

The positions of the valves within the sub-districts have a twofold object. They are arranged so as to separate the sub-districts into a series of sections, or, as they are termed, "shuts," for the purpose of inspection by waste water-meter, and they enable any particular section to be turned off for service connections or repairs without having to turn the whole of a sub-district off.

Considering them first from the point of view of the waste-water meter inspection. It will be seen by the Diagram No. 14 of No. 5 sub-district, which is taken as our example, that there are eight separate "shuts" or sections thereon.

It is not intended here to deal at any length with the details in relation to waste water-meter inspection ; but some particulars are necessary to explain the arranging of the valves.

I would refer those who are desirous of studying the subject fully, to the paper on " The Constant Supply and

DIAGRAM No. 14.

ENLARGEMENT OF
SUB-DISTRICT Nº 5

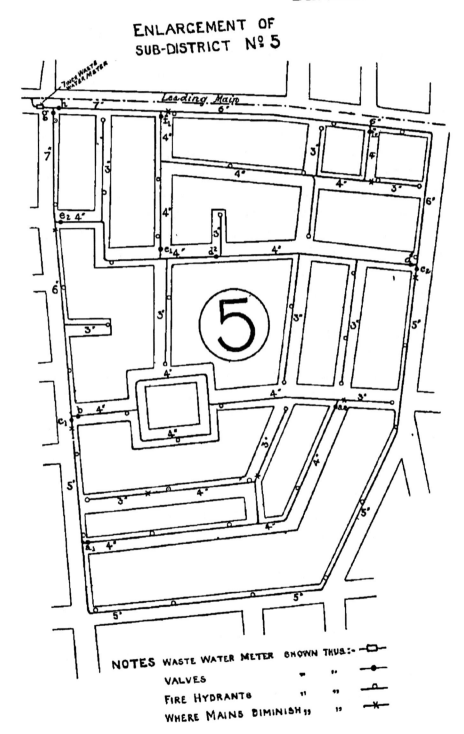

NOTES WASTE WATER METER SHOWN THUS:- ▭
         VALVES   "   "   ●
         FIRE HYDRANTS   "   "   ○
         WHERE MAINS DIMINISH " "   ✳

Waste of Water," read by Mr Geo. F. Deacon, M.Inst.
C.E. (the inventor of the waste water-meter bearing his
name), before the Society of Arts in May 1882. This
paper, which has been reprinted and issued by the makers
of the Deacon meter, deals exhaustively with the waste-
detecting system, and is illustrated by diagrams of
inspection, and sections of the meter.

With such a sub-district or waste water-meter district
as our example, if the waste water-meter shows that a
large quantity of water is going at night, indicative of
waste, the first thing to be done is to night inspect the
said district ; and here the purpose of the valves from a
waste water-meter point of view comes in, by enabling
the waste to be located.

The waste line recorded upon diagram by the indicating apparatus of the waste water-meter should not
exceed 600 gallons an hour by night, equal to a rate per
twenty-four hours of about 5 gallons per head for the
population of 3,000 in the sub-district.

If the waste line is high, and it is decided to night
inspect the district, a clean diagram paper is put upon
the recording drum of waste water-meter. This drum is
moved by clockwork, and makes one complete revolution
in twenty-four hours, or in a special form of apparatus
for night inspection purposes, once in six hours. The
pencil, actuated by displacement due to the rate of water
passing, will, if no water is passing, show a line upon
diagram paper at zero, or will show whatever amouut
of water is going. The action of the meter will be
described in a later chapter.

Representative diagrams Nos. 15 and 16 are appended,
No. 15 showing the meter diagram in full with the day
and night flow, and No. 16 showing on a larger scale a
portion of the diagram for the night-time, with a series
of "shuts off" and the effect they have in lowering the

line of flow, the final shut on the meter valve bringing the line down to zero.

The night inspection having been decided upon, the waste inspectors will arrange the time for the "shuts off." The various sections of the sub-district will be shut off at equal intervals of time, and afterwards re-opened, and by subsequent reference to the meter diagram, the amount of flow shut off upon each section will be at once apparent. Those shuts upon which the waste is found to occur will be further dealt with.

The order in which the shuts are made is by working back from the extremity of the sub-district to the meter on the leading branch main, the meter valve being the last shut.

In the example, the first shut will be valves a_1 and a_2, the second shut will be valve b; the third shut will be c_1 and c_2, the fourth shut will be d^1 and d^2; the fifth shut will be e_1 and e_2; the sixth shut will be f_1 and f_2, the seventh shut will be g; and eighth shut h. The valve of the waste water-meter could be substituted for either g or h for the last shut; but there is a special reason for fixing the valves on each branch in the positions shown, which will be pointed out a little later on.

Those shuts upon which the waste is found to occur will be set apart to be further dealt with, for location of the waste, according to the methods set forth in the paper before referred to.

The valves employed for the "shuts off" on the various sections are of great service for the purpose of connections and repairs to service pipes, and in the event of burst mains, as by their use it is only necessary to turn off a small part of the supply at a time. A careful arrangement of the position of the valves is necessary for this purpose. It has been mentioned that either of the valves g or h could be done away with, the meter

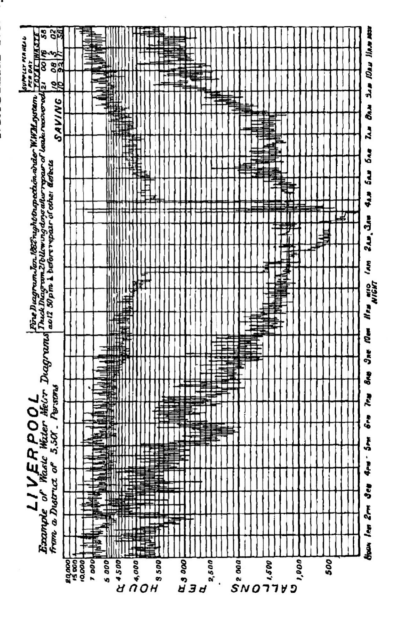

DIAGRAM No. 15.

LIVERPOOL
Example of Waste Water Meter Diagrams
from a District of 5,500 Persons

Fine Diagram Jan. 1882 night inspection under W.W.M. system.
Thick Diagram 27 following days after repair of leaks recovered
ao 12.50 p.m. & before repair of other defects

SAVING

	SUPPLY PER HEAD PER DAY	TOTAL WASTE
	21	00	16	58
	10	08	3	02
	10	92	7	56

GALLONS PER HOUR

20,000
15,000
10,000
7,000
5,000
4,500
4,000
3,500
3,000
2,500
2,000
1,500
1,000
500

Noon 1pm 2pm 3pm 4pm 5pm 6pm 7pm 8pm 9pm 10pm 11pm mid 1am 2am 3am 4am 5am 6am 7am 8am 9am 10am 11am noon
NIGHT

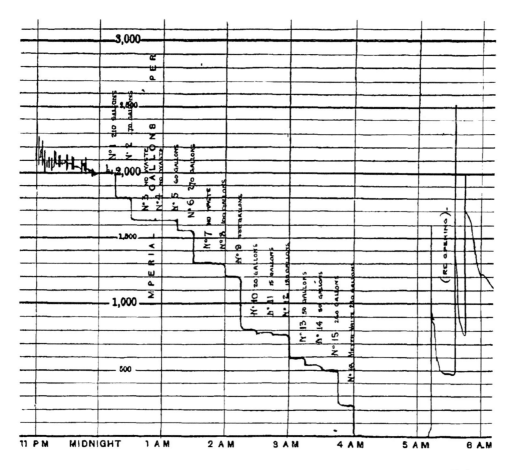

valve taking its place for the last "shut off" on the sub-district; but they are arranged so for the purposes just mentioned. Supposing the water has to be off on either of the leading 7-inch branches running south or east; if on the branch running east, valve h would be shut, and the water would only be off on the main running from h to c_2—the water would be served to the whole of the rest of the district through valve g; the valves f_1, f_2, d^1, and c_2 would of course be shut, and it is easily seen by examining diagram that this would be so, it was also with this end in view that valve e_1 was inserted, and the main connected at that point, rather than for the waste water-meter purposes. For the same reason, valves c_1 and c_2 have been fixed in the positions shown; if, for instance, a burst occurred on the 6-inch main running south past valve c_1, the only main that would have to be off for repairs would be between valves c_1 and c_2, which would be shut, also a_1. Broadly speaking, it is a good rule, wherever a main branches in two directions, to put a valve on each branch, just past the junction, so that according to whichever main has to be off, the valve commanding it can be shut, and the water turned round the other way.

From what has been said, it will be seen that it is necessary to consider jointly the requirements of the waste water-meter shuts, and the question of turning off the least possible amount in case of connections or repairs.

The position of the fire-hydrants in the roadways has been discussed in the previous chapter. As regards their distance apart, the statutory obligations of a water undertaking generally require that they shall be fixed not more than a certain distance from one another; generally the greatest distance between them must not exceed 100 yards.

The next and very important point to determine is the sizes of the distributing pipes. It was considered advisable, however, to deal with the arrangement of the pipes and valves first, as the relative sizes of the main depends to a large extent upon the way in which they are connected up for circulation.

It will be understood that the example chart, and the sizes determined for the mains to the sub-districts shown thereon, are only for the purpose of illustration, and where in actual practice the size and population of the districts differ from same, the sizes would vary accordingly.

Taking enlargement of sub-district No. 5 in detail for sizes. The leading branch main is 7-inch, for the reasons before assigned, and this will of course require a 7-inch waste water-meter. The full size of 7 inches is given to the branches running south and east, until the first sections or "shuts" junctioning from them are passed; this is considered advisable because in case of the water having to be turned off as before referred to on either leg, the full supply to the whole of the sub-district will have to be served through the other leg or branch main. The mains running south and east, after passing the first junctions, will diminish to 6-inch, and afterwards to 5-inch, as shown; the said branches ultimately unite and encircle the whole of the sub-district; it is not therefore considered advisable to diminish them below 5-inch, as they are what may be termed the main arteries to the sub-district. The remainder of the distributing mains within the sub-district will be 4 inches and 3 inches in diameter, as shown upon diagram. The process of calculation employed for the leading mains throughout the high and low level zones, and for the leading branches to the sub-districts, cannot be carried further with any advantage.

Within each sub-district the sizes of the mains will be reduced as necessary, according to how they are branched and connected; the aim being to properly distribute the full supply led into the sub-districts, throughout the distributing pipes.

In the diagram of sub-district No. 5, the sizes have been apportioned to suit that example, and the circumstances of each case must be considered, and the sizes of the mains arranged accordingly.

The prevailing sizes recommended for the general distributing pipes are 4 inches and 3 inches in diameter.

The reason why the calculations employed for the leading mains are not applicable to the general rank and file of the distributing pipes is because the aggregate area of the smaller pipes must be in excess of the area of the leading branches in all sub-districts where the distributing pipes are numerous for a network of streets. This must necessarily be so. For example, a sub-district having a leading branch entering it, of 6 inches diameter, to supply the maximum rate per head over the whole sub-district, may have the mains ultimately branched up into twenty different streets, the diameter for the main in each street for its proportional discharge would be about $1\frac{3}{4}$ inches, which is altogether inadequate.

The 6-inch diameter for the leader is sufficient for the maximum rate of draught spread over the whole of the sub-district, but a large proportion of the total is liable to be localised in any particular part.

In the first place, the domestic supply is variable; out of the aggregate amount drawn in the sub-district, the draught may be much heavier at one part than another at various periods.

In the second place, there may require to be extra large supplies taken off the distributing pipes at certain points for trade purposes, the draught upon which will occasionally be very heavy. It is impossible to tell, when laying out the distributing pipes, where these special supplies may be wanted, so that if the main area of the distributing pipes was restricted to their theoretical carrying capacities for the domestic requirements only, they would not be of sufficient area to meet any special supplies.

In the third place, the distributing pipes, if less than 3 inches in diameter, would be inadequate for fire purposes. This is a point of such vital importance, that upon it hinges the whole question of the sizes of the general distributing pipes, because if they are of the necessary area for an efficient fire supply, they will be large enough to fulfil all other requirements.

In briefly concluding this chapter, the author would remark that although the sub-districts in example chart vary greatly in character, it does not appear to be necessary to give any further enlargements of typical districts, as the explanation would involve a good deal of repetition without adding much information; and the only interest the chart has for us is to serve as an example of the details and general outlines of distribution.

It may be well, however, to point out that in outlying districts, where there are but few roads, and those are long and straggling, it will be well to keep the mains of larger diameter until they approach the terminals, because although the mains are larger, the aggregate main area will be no greater, and the circulation will be poorer than in the more compact districts where the roads are shorter and more numerous, with frequent junctions, and the mains consequently in better circulation. Moreover, in the long roads the friction on the long lengths of pipe will be very considerable, and the fire-hydrants occurring every 80 or 100 yards, will be liable, in case of fire, to be a very heavy tax on a single long length of distributing pipe. In such a case as sub-district No. 14 on chart the main areas should be well maintained for the reasons given.

The sizes suitable in this instance being indicated upon chart, which will dispense with the occasion for a separate enlargement, except in this particular case, the sizes for the distributing mains have, for the sake of clearness, been omitted from the chart

But as sub-districts Nos. 5 and 14 are typical of the two extremes, or opposite character of districts, it is thought that they will sufficiently indicate the mode of procedure.

The fire-hydrants, except those upon the ends of mains, are omitted from chart, but are shown upon the enlargement of sub-district No. 5, and as the distances apart at which they should occur have been stated, it has been deemed superfluous to mark them upon chart.

The fire-hydrants are generally from $1\frac{1}{2}$ to $2\frac{1}{2}$ inches in diameter in the water-way, and their discharge varies very much according to circumstances.

A 2-inch fire-hydrant drawing a fair supply from a 3-inch main will probably deliver from 3,000 to 5,000 gallons an hour, providing it has a free outlet, and the full capacity of the main; and therefore the total available head is utilised in overcoming friction.

This may only be allowed when the supply is delivered into a receiving tank, at ground level, for the steam fire-engine to pump from.

Where, on the other hand, it is required to play a jet on the fire by means of a hose direct from the hydrant, the discharge must be restricted by the employment of a hand-pipe and nozzle on the end of the hose.

It must not be supposed, from anything that has been said, that the essential object of a discharge nozzle is to restrict the flow; its primary object is to give a good jet to the greatest possible height, the velocity of the water passing through the nozzle is accelerated, and it issues in a compact jet, to which the air offers the least resistance, so that with a well-constructed nozzle, the size of which is properly apportioned to the head and quantity of water passing, the height the jet attains very nearly approaches the head of water on jet.

This subject is admirably dealt with in Mr Thomas Box's Treatise on Hydraulics.

But where the nozzle is employed at the end of a long main, as in the case of a fire-hydrant supply, to quote Mr Box's words, "Calculation must be made of the loss of head by friction in such pipes so as to obtain the actual head on the jet." If, therefore, the main is discharging its maximum, the whole of the head will be expended in overcoming friction, and there will be no head available on the jet. This point has been emphasised in order to make it clear that the regulation of the size of the nozzle is necessary to restrict the flow and ensure a head on the jet.

Extra large sized fire-hydrants are sometimes fixed upon the leading mains where they run in close proximity to the important warehouses and public buildings These supplementary fire supplies, which are additional to the hydrants upon the distributing mains, are of great service in case of outbreaks of fire upon an extensive scale, as they furnish an immense volume of water for use in connection with the steam fire-engines.

There are sundry other accessories in connection with water supply and distribution that require a short notice.

Perhaps the most important is the question of air-escapes.

The supply mains from the sources, and the pumping mains that run a long distance with no outlets or junctions off them, require to be well provisioned with air-escapes, which should be fixed on every summit or anticlinal, and be of an approved self-acting type. In connection with each of these there should be an air-pipe of about $\frac{3}{4}$ or 1 inch diameter, with a full way-cock on same, to be worked by hand to assist in letting large quantities of air off, when a main is being charged after emptying. The leading mains to the distributing systems should also be furnished with self-acting air-escapes, and with the air-pipes to be worked by hand.

The author considers that air-escapes are practically unnecessary upon the distributing mains in the sub-districts, his experience being that there is no difficulty in this direction, the supplies off the distributing pipes acting as ample provision for the escape of air.

Wash-outs are very necessary upon the trunk mains for either gravitation or pumping supplies, and also upon the large leading mains to the systems of distribution. Upon the distributing mains the hydrants act as wash-outs.

Pressure-reducing valves or break-pressure tanks are not often necessary. They may, however, be occasionally required, where, for instance, the sources of supply are at a great altitude, and deliver direct into the system of distribution without the intervention of reservoirs, especially where the district has great variations of levels.

CHAPTER IV.

PIPES AND FITTINGS UPON DISTRIBUTING SYSTEM.

SOME account will be given in this chapter of the pipes, valves, and other apparatus and fittings connected with a system of distribution.

It is as well perhaps to remark, in opening the chapter, that the illustrations which will be given are in order only to make the text clear. The very elaborate catalogues prepared by the best hydraulic makers are so complete that it would be quite superfluous to multiply examples in this treatise. What will be aimed at will be, a concise account, illustrated where necessary by distinctive types of the pipes, valves, and various fittings necessary for a first-class system of distribution.

Cast-Iron Pipes and Irregulars.—The pipes employed for the leading and distributing mains will be first dealt with.

A brief description will suffice of the cast-iron pipes suitable for waterwork distribution, usage and long experience having settled the most convenient form for the straight pipes and irregular castings. Descriptions of the proportions and strength of pipes are given in many hydraulic and engineering works Molesworth's admirable pocket-book of " Engineering Formulæ " gives complete tables of the thickness and weight of pipes for various working heads, also the best proportions for the sockets, and handy formulæ for calculating the strength and thickness. Proportions and thickness for water pipes are also given in Box's treatise on hydraulics and in other publications, and Messrs Taylor, in their publication, referred to in the last chapter, give the necessary thickness of pipes in a very convenient diagram form, which can be recommended to engineers who want a handy reference for frequent use. There are so many sources of information that the author considers it unnecessary to labour this short treatise with a lot of tables and particulars on the subject.

All cast-iron pipes should be proved by being subjected to a stress before leaving the foundry where they are cast, equal to double the working head for which they are intended, which should be sustained for several minutes, during which time they should be repeatedly struck with a hand hammer to produce a strong vibration of the pipes.

Test specimen bars and rods of the metal employed in casting the pipes should be submitted by the founders for test purposes, for transverse and tensile strength.

It is also important that the metal in the bodies of the pipes should be of uniform thickness, and that the weights should not vary beyond a certain range, usually from 3 per cent. to 4 per cent. in the smaller diameter pipes for distribution.

The straight pipes should be cast in sand moulds set vertically, and the irregular castings in close boxes

The pipes are generally coated before leaving the foundry, both externally and internally, with Dr Angus Smith's composition, as a preventative against rust. This is done immediately after the pipes are proved, and before they are attacked by rust; they are heated to 300° to 400° F., and are then dipped in a nearly boiling mixture of the composition, which forms a hard glaze upon the surface of the metal.

The pipes for a system of distribution, where the statical heads range up to 200 feet, as in our example, should be tested to a proof strain of not less than 600 feet, because, although the statical head does not exceed 200 feet, something higher than that should be taken as the working head on account of the various stresses to which the pipes are liable in their lifetime. The two principal dangers are: first, the chance of air becoming entangled in the pipes, which will be likely to give rise to shock or "hammering" in the pipes; and second, turning the water on and off suddenly, for under the strictest supervision it will sometimes happen that the valves will be turned off too hurriedly, which, by suddenly arresting the flow of water, will give rise to concussion. There is also the stress to which the pipes are subjected by earth movement and heavy traffic, although this is minimised by proper precautions as before explained.

At any rate the working pressure may well be taken at 300 feet, requiring a proof strain of 600 feet as before stated.

The thickness of metal for the bodies of the pipes for this head is given by Molesworth's Tables as follows :—

2-inch bore pipe	$\frac{3}{8}$-inch thickness.	
3 ,, ,,	$\frac{3}{8}$,,	,,
4 ,, ,,	$\frac{3}{8}$,,	,,
5 ,, ,,	$\frac{13}{32}$,,	,,
6 ,, ,,	$\frac{7}{16}$,,	,,
7 ,, ,,	$\frac{1}{2}$,,	,,
8 ,, ,,	$\frac{1}{2}$,,	,,
9 ,, ,,	$\frac{9}{16}$,,	,,
10 ,, ,,	$\frac{9}{16}$,,	,,
12 ,, ,,	$\frac{9}{16}$,,	,,

The weights per 9 feet pipe, and per foot run, and other particulars, are also given *in extenso* in Molesworth's Tables, in which are handy formulæ for obtaining the weight and strength.

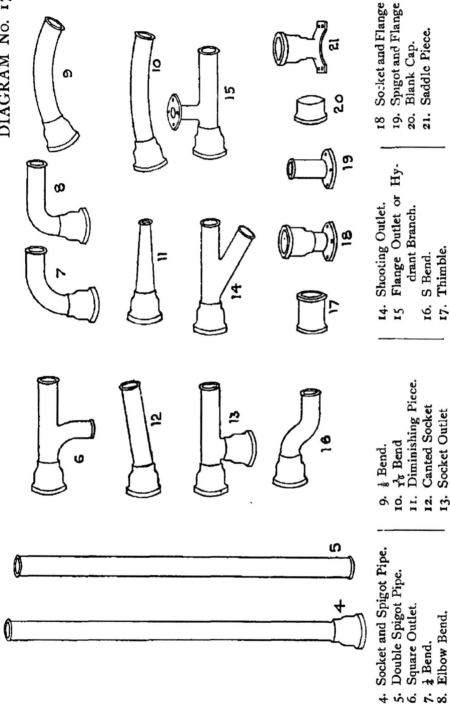

DIAGRAM No. 17.

4. Socket and Spigot Pipe.
5. Double Spigot Pipe,
6. Square Outlet.
7. ¼ Bend.
8. Elbow Bend.

9. ⅛ Bend.
10. 1⁄16 Bend
11. Diminishing Piece.
12. Canted Socket
13. Socket Outlet

14. Shooting Outlet.
15. Flange Outlet or Hy-
     drant Branch.
16. S Bend.
17. Thimble.

18. Socket and Flange Piece
19. Spigot and Flange Piece
20. Blank Cap.
21. Saddle Piece.

There is another consideration to be taken account of in determining the necessary strength and thickness of pipes, and that is their probable deterioration in the ground. All pipes are more or less liable to decay in the process of time according to the conditions to which they are ordinarily subject. Very soft waters tend to rapidly decompose the pipes by oxidisation, and externally they are more or less subject to corrosion, due to dampness, and the nature of the soil.* Taking everything into consideration, it is often deemed advisable to make the distributing pipes slightly stouter than the calculated thickness for a working head of 300 feet.

The following is a table of thickness and weights for distributing pipes from 2 inches to 12 inches in diameter.

Internal Diameter	†Length over all (include Socket)		Thickness nf Metal	Weight of Pipe.		
inches	ft.	in.	inch	Cwts.	qrs.	lbs.
2	6	3	$\frac{3}{8}$	0	2	4
3	9	$3\frac{1}{2}$	$\frac{3}{8}$ full	1	1	0
4	9	4	$\frac{7}{16}$	1	2	20
5	9	$4\frac{1}{2}$	$\frac{7}{16}$ full	2	1	10
6	9	$4\frac{1}{2}$	$\frac{1}{2}$ full	3	0	6
7	9	$4\frac{1}{2}$	$\frac{9}{16}$	3	2	24
8	9	$4\frac{1}{2}$	$\frac{5}{8}$ bare	4	1	20
9	9	$4\frac{1}{2}$	$\frac{5}{8}$	5	1	1
10	9	$4\frac{1}{2}$	$\frac{11}{16}$	6	1	20
12 {	9	$4\frac{1}{2}$	$\frac{11}{16}$ full	7	3	0
	12	$4\frac{1}{2}$	$\frac{11}{16}$ full	10	0	0

* Carbonaceous matter—cinders, for instance—will, with any moisture, eat into the iron if laid against pipes

† The lengths given include the lengths of the sockets, so that the pipes when laid and jointed measure 6, 9, or 12 feet (as the case may be) from joint to joint.

In addition to the straight pipes, there are the double spigot pipes for repairs, also the branches (or outlets), bends, canted socket pipes, diminishing pipes, hydrant branches, socket and flange pipes, thimbles, blank caps, etc.

The pipes and various irregulars are shown by Figs. 4 to 21, on Diagram No. 17.

One rule which must be observed upon a system of distribution, if endless confusion is to be avoided, is to adopt a set of standard dimensions for all pipes and irregulars, and adhere rigidly to same. It is a practical impossibility to differentiate the thickness of the pipes in the district of supply according to the varying pressures.

The sockets of all pipes and irregulars must be carefully kept to standard dimensions as well as the thickness of the bodies of the pipes, so that whenever repairs or connections have to be made, the spigots may fit the sockets and thimble-joints properly.

The best thing to do with any old or obsolete patterns is to break them up for scrap as quickly as possible. No one but those who have experienced it know the trouble that may be caused by finding at the last moment that a spigot is too big for the socket. When this happens, perhaps in the dead of the night, after the water has already been off for some time, and it means waiting a couple of hours longer until a fresh pipe or irregular is fetched, it is little short of a calamity.

The general proportions of the sockets are given in Molesworth's Tables, and sections are there shown of lead-joints and of turned and bored joints. It is not intended here to repeat the tables of proportions of the sockets. Sections will, however, be given of ordinary and special forms of socket-joints. Fig. 22 is a section of an ordinary form of socket-joint. The annular jointing space is about $\frac{5}{16}$ to $\frac{3}{8}$ inch; the joint is caulked with yarn, leaving a depth of about 2½ inches, which is run with lead and then set up.

This is a very good joint for general distributing pipes and irregulars, and if there is a proper depth of lead, and it is well set up, there is little likelihood of the joint leaking

Fig. 23 is another type of joint very suitable where

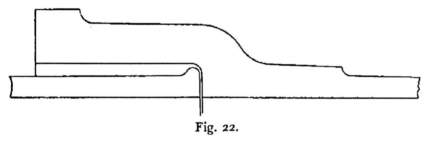

Fig. 22.

laying long lengths of main, as it does away with the use of yarn ; there is a deeper rim on the end of the spigot, and an annular recess in the interior of socket. With this type instead of yarn the joint is caulked with strip lead of the section shown, after which the joint is run solid with lead and set up in the usual way. The recess in the socket is to make the lead-joint more secure.

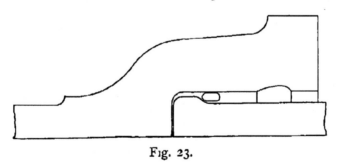

Fig. 23.

Fig 24 is another type of socket which can be caulked with strip lead, and makes a very secure joint.

Fig 25 is a turned and bored joint. These are not often employed for water supply, and are only used where the pipes are laid in perfectly uniform lines through a subway, or where special provision is made for them.

Lead-Jointing —The lead for jointing the pipes should
be the best soft blue pig lead, and the joint should be
run in one running. In the case of a large pipe joint
two ladles will have to be used, pouring with both at the
same time, so as to ensure the whole of the lead being
run in together in a liquid state.

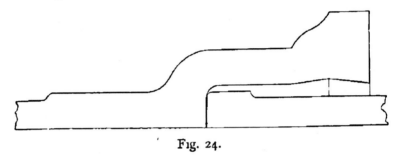

Fig. 24.

For pouring the lead into the joint, a gasket of platted
yarn or clay on the smaller pipes is wound round the
pipe close to the front of the socket-joint, and the lead
poured into an opening at the top. Instead of the platted
yarn a special form of clip is sometimes employed (see
Fig. 26), which is very convenient for the purpose.

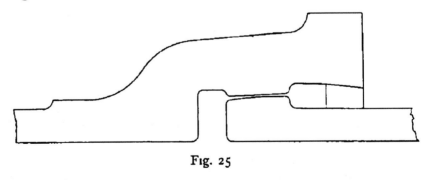

Fig. 25

Nicholson's patent combined melting pot and ladle,
shown by Figs. 27 and 28, is very convenient for running
the lead joints. It has a valve in the bottom worked by
a spindle and lever The lead is melted in the ladle
itself, which is then slung over the pipe-joint, and the

valve raised, allowing the necessary quantity of lead to run into the joint.

Sluice Valves. — The sluice-valves or turn-off valves, which are termed "gates" in the United States, are a very important item in a distributing system, a very large number having to be employed upon the leading and distributing mains. Fig. 29 is a section of the usual form of sluice - valves. The valves should be double-faced, having four gun-metal faces, two on body of valve and two on valve door, as shown

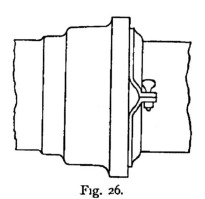

Fig. 26.

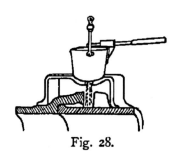

Fig. 28.

The valve spindle and nut are of gun-metal, and the gland and stuffing-box should be bushed with gun-metal.

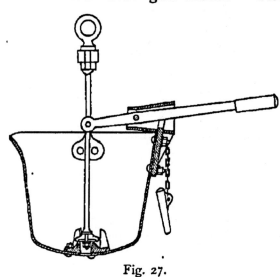

Fig. 27.

The valves may have socket or flanged ends as desired. It will be seen that the spindle has a left-handed thread, in order that the valve may be what is termed right-handed, that is, that the valve door shall open by turning from left to right.

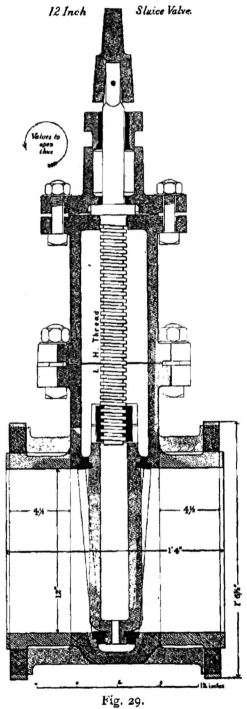

Fig. 29.

All valves should be proved to a hydrostatic pressure, due to a column of water 600 feet in altitude, and should be coated with Dr Angus Smith's patent composition

The advantage of a screw-down valve is that it cannot be closed very suddenly, as it requires several turns of the spindle to close or open. Even this form of valve, however, should not be opened or closed too quickly.

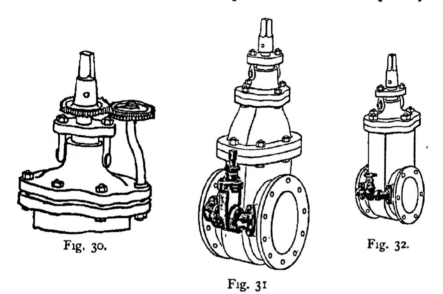

Fig. 30.   Fig. 32.

Fig. 31

Plug-cocks should not be allowed under any circumstances upon the iron pipes, as their sudden closing would be disastrous.

A very important point to be observed is, that all sluice-valves should open the same way. Where some are right-handed and others left-handed valves, in a district of supply, a lot of trouble is likely to be caused through the valves being left closed by mistake.

It is well with large valves upon leading mains to have indicating wheel gearing, arranged to show when they are full open, or only partly open, or closed. Fig. 30 is a type of such an arrangement.

A very useful attachment for large sluice-valves is a small by-pass arrangement with a turn-off valve (see Fig. 31), or stop-cock (see Fig. 32), upon same, for charging up the main after emptying, as it is very difficult to start opening the door of a big sluice-valve when the pressure is on one side only. Gearing is sometimes used for working large valves (see Fig. 33), and it is also convenient sometimes to employ bevel gearing (see Fig.

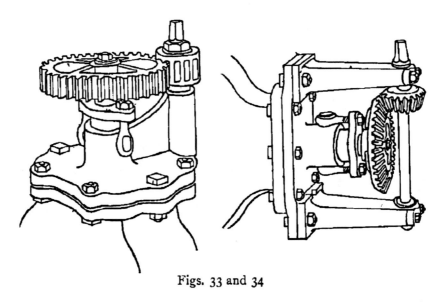

Figs. 33 and 34

34), for working valves where the valves have to be laid on their sides.

Wash-Outs.—Sluice-valves are also used as wash-outs and for draining the leading mains. In this case a branch pipe is laid from the main, and the sluice-valve fixed upon same to drain into a street gully, or water-course, or other suitable place.

Air-Escapes.—Fig. 35 is a self-acting single air-valve, with a floating ball, to act under pressure, and allow the small quantities of air to escape which occasionally accumulate on the summits of pipe lines.

Fig. 36 is a type of double air-valve. The ball on the right acts under pressure, allowing the small quantities of air that accumulate to escape through the small orifice, the same as the self-acting single air-valve. The large aperture on the left is intended for the escape of the large quantities of air while the pipes are being filled with water, the floating ball closing same when the main is fully charged with water.

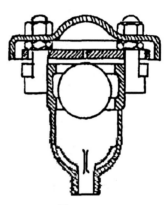

Fig. 35.

There are also triple ball air-escapes, the centre ball acting under pressure and allowing the small quantities of air that accumulate to escape, while the two large apertures, one on each side of the centre one, are for the escape of large volumes of air.

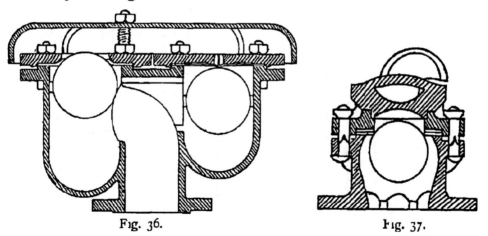

Fig. 36.   Fig. 37.

Fire-Hydrants.—Coming next to fire-hydrants, we find "their name is legion," the various hydraulic makers vying with each other in producing the most

suitable and convenient patterns. I believe the earliest
type was Bateman & Moore's patent fire-hydrant, or fire-
cock (see Fig 37), origin-
ally manufactured solely
by Messrs Guest &
Chrimes. The patent has
long since run out, but
this form of fire-hydrant
still holds its own as a
cheap and efficient valve.
It is opened by the application of a stand-pipe
(see Fig 38) which has a
screwed spindle working
through a stuffing-box,
with a cup on the bottom
that depresses the ball-
valve and allows the free
passage of the water up-
wards through the tube
of stand-pipe.

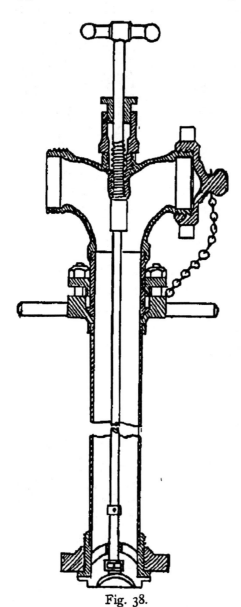

Fig. 38.

This hydrant can be
fixed directly upon a line
of main by means of a
hydrant branch (see Fig.
15, Diagram No. 17, of
pipes and irregulars), or
it can be fixed upon the
end of a main or branch
by means of a socket
elbow (see Fig. 39).

This hydrant is also a
self-acting air-discharger,
which is of considerable advantage when filling mains.

There are many patterns of loose-valve and sluice-

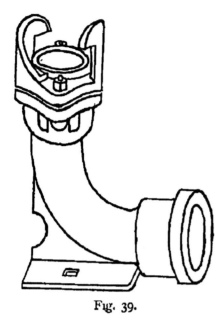

Fig. 39.

valve screw-down hydrants. Fig. 40, known as the Brighton pattern, manufactured by Messrs J. Stone & Co., is a type of loose-valve screw-down hydrant with gun-metal screwed outlet for stand-pipe; this pattern hydrant fixes on top of the main.

Fig. 41 is another pattern manufactured by Messrs Guest & Chrimes; it has a bayonet-joint connection for stand-pipe, and fixes on the side or end of main. Fig. 42 is a sluice-valve hydrant which gives a clear water-way. This hydrant has a gun-metal screwed outlet for stand-pipe.

The screw-down hydrants can have either the gun-metal screwed outlet or the bayonet joint, as may be desired, for attaching stand-pipe.

The hydrants, besides being used for fire purposes, serve as wash-outs, and for draining the mains, and by leaving them slightly open when charging a main they assist the escape of air.

There are many other excellent pat-

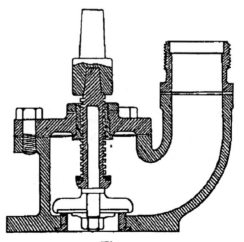

Fig. 40.

terns by the various hydraulic makers, but space will
not permit of further examples being shown.

Fire-hydrants for internal fire-fittings, or mill-valves
as they are generally termed, are shown of various
patterns by Figs. 43 to 47.

The sizes for the ordinary road hydrants, and of those
for internal use, vary from $1\frac{1}{2}$ to $2\frac{1}{2}$ inches diameter in
the bore.

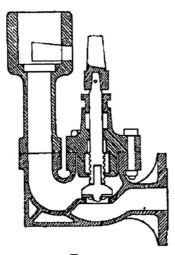

Fig. 41.

Where, however, it is desired to put fire-hydrants
upon the leading mains in the
central districts for very large
volumes of water, especially
for the supply of the steam
fire-engines, 3-inch diameter
clear-way sluice-valve hydrants
are very suitable, similar in
pattern to Fig. 42 before
given.

Injector Hydrant. — Mr
Greathead's injector hydrant is
a very ingenious apparatus
whereby a small jet of high-
pressure water, injected into a
large jet from the waterworks main, intensifies the pressure of the latter in the delivery hose. This apparatus, which is shown by Fig. 48, was illustrated and
described in Mr E. B Ellington's paper upon Hydraulic
Power in London, read before the Institution of Civil
Engineers.*

By its use, wherever hydraulic power mains are laid,
a jet of great power can be obtained at the top of the
highest buildings without the intervention of fire-
engines.

---

* Minutes of Proc. Inst. Civil Engineers, vol. xciv.

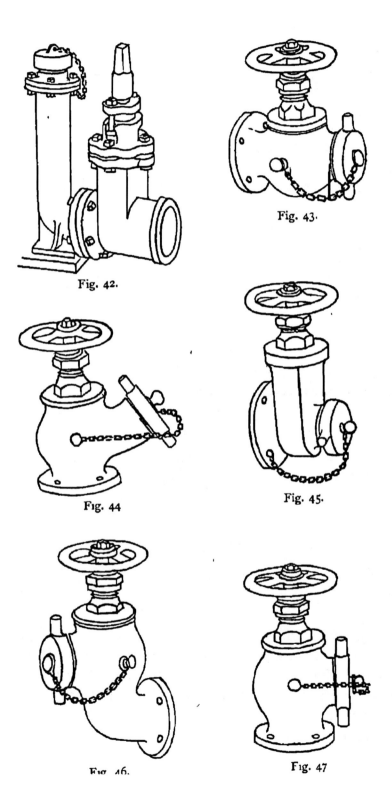

Fig. 42.

Fig. 43.

Fig. 44

Fig. 45.

Fig. 46.

Fig. 47

STAND-PIPES AND HOSE ATTACHMENTS AND NOZZLES FOR FIRE-HYDRANTS.

Stand-Pipes.—One form of stand-pipe has been shown by Fig. 38 in connection with the Bateman & Moore fire-hydrant, which has a double outlet. Similar stand-pipes are used with the other forms of fire-hydrants for street use, only omitting the screw-spindle and cup

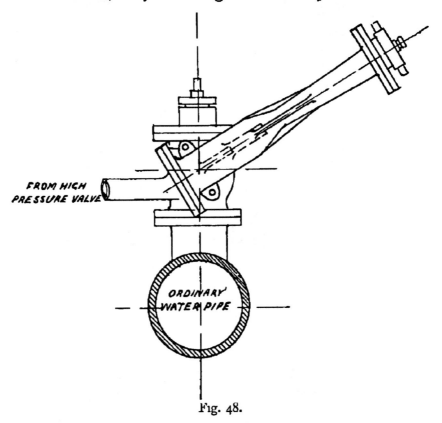

Fig. 48.

arrangement that was required with the ball-hydrant Fig. 49 is a stand-pipe with a single outlet. It will be noticed that the stand-pipes have stuffing-boxes and revolving heads, which is a useful provision to enable the outlets to be turned in whatever direction the hose is required to discharge.

Stand-pipes are used for other purposes as well as in case of fires. They are employed for shipping, for the supply of ships' tanks; and occasionally for other supplies for trade purposes. When this is the case, a meter is generally attached to the outlet of the stand-pipe through which the water can be registered.

It is well for the waterworks department to keep a number of stand-pipes in stock, so that in case of very severe frost, should a number of consumers' supplies be frozen, the stand-pipes can be fixed upon the fire-hydrants, and a supply obtained in such manner for domestic use, screw-down bib-cocks being fitted to the hydrants for this purpose. The same stand-pipes can be used for ordinary purposes at any other time, the bib-cocks having been removed, and blank ferrules inserted, and for taking main pressures at any time, it is only necessary to remove the blank ferrule and screw on the pressure-gauge.

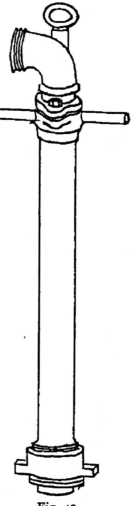

Fig. 49.

Fire-Hose.—The hose may be either indiarubber, leather, or canvas. The copper-riveted leather hose is the most expensive, but is very durable; canvas hose is light, and very convenient for transporting upon hand-reel or fire-engine; the india-rubber hose is very suitable, but it must be looked after carefully, as it is very easily injured, and is liable to deteriorate after it has been exposed to the light for some time. It is preserved best in a dark place, or when immersed in water.

Hose-Couplings. — The ordinary form of hose-couplings is shown by Fig. 50. There are also several varieties of patent instantaneous couplings, which may be found advertised, that are very convenient.

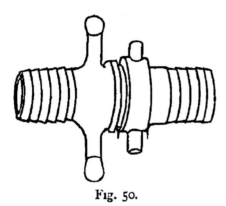

Fig. 50.

Hand-Pipe and Nozzle or Jet.—Fig. 51 shows a hand-pipe, and Fig. 52 a nozzle or jet, for attachment to end of hand-pipe The purpose of these has been already dealt with in the previous chapter. The size for general use, for the hand-pipe, is 2 feet to 2 feet 6 inches long, tapered in the internal diameter from $2\frac{1}{2}$ inches to $1\frac{1}{2}$ inches. The nozzles or jets vary in size. For fire-brigade purposes a set of nozzles are kept ready for use. The sizes generally used for a direct supply from the

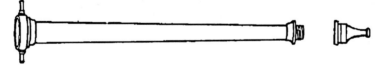

Figs. 51 and 52

water-mains are from $\frac{1}{2}$ to $\frac{7}{8}$ inch in diameter at outlet; it is not often that the larger of these diameters will afford a strong enough jet of water, and the smaller ones have to be used, whereby the flow is restricted; but a better head is available, and the jet is projected with greater force and much better effect to " hit " the fire out, as it is sometimes expressed. Where the supply from one or more fire-hydrants is delivered at ground level into the receiving tank for the steam fire-engine. or from one of the large full-way hydrants off the leading main, the supply thus obtained is pumped under a pressure of about 100 lbs. to the square inch, and as the head due to this pressure is all available at the jet, the

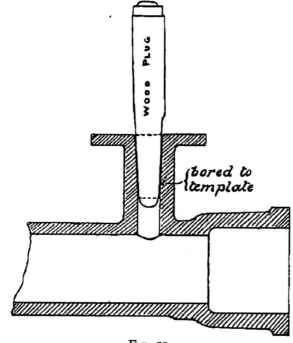

WOOD PLUG

bored to
template

Fig. 53.

nozzle is not required to restrict the flow, and a larger size can be employed, probably $1\frac{1}{4}$ inches at the outlet.

Fire-Plugs, as shown by Fig. 53, are sometimes employed instead of the fire-hydrants upon the distributing mains, as a provision for fire purposes. These are elm-wood plugs tapered at one end, and driven into orifices in the fire-plug branches, which are fixed upon the lines of mains. The orifices are bored out taper, and the wood plugs are driven in by the butt end of the bar carried by the workman. To draw a plug, the pointed end of the bar is driven into the top, which is prevented from splitting by a wrought-iron ring. By shaking the plug with the bar it is soon loosened, and the pressure of the water assists in drawing it out. The stand-pipes for use where fire-plugs occur have tapered ends, and are driven into the orifices in the fire-plug branches.

Fire-hydrants should always be fixed in preference to fire-plugs upon main ends, because they can be opened and closed at will for flushing out the pipes without turning the mains off

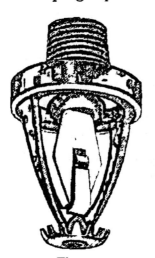

Fig. 54.

Automatic Sprinkler and Fire Alarm. — Sprinklers are rapidly growing in public favour for fire extinction in mills and factories. The sprinkler installation consists of a number of what are termed "sprinklers," the action of which is somewhat on the same lines as the fusible plugs in boilers. .The "sprinklers" are attached in rows to a series of water-pipes laid along under the ceilings of the rooms or warehouses it is desired to protect.*

The apertures in sprinklers for the escape of water are closed by valves, which are kept in place by fastenings held by a metal alloy which fuses at a comparatively low temperature. Upon the outbreak of fire in a warehouse provided with a "sprinkler" installation, as soon as the heat rises to the melting-point of the metal alloy,

---

* A general view of a Grinnell sprinkler is shown by Fig. 54.

the sprinklers come into action, and the whole of the warehouse is subjected to a downpour of water from the ranges of sprinklers, which effectually extinguishes the fire before it has time to obtain a hold upon the premises. It is essential that the supply to the sprinklers shall not be liable to be turned off, and it is generally considered advisable to have alternative supplies to provide against any chance of failure, so that it is desirable to connect all sprinkler installations to leading mains which are not turned off for district purposes, and, if possible, to two such mains separately supplied, in order that if one is off on account of accident or repairs, the other may be available. Back pressure valves are placed on the branch pipes from each supply to close automatically against either main, the supply from which may chance to fail.

Where only one main is available for supplying the sprinkler installation, it is usual to provide a tank or water-tower at the top of the building as an alternative supply, but in this case some reliable means must be adopted to prevent any chance of the water from the tower getting back into the water-mains, when the pressure in them is less than the head on tower.

That the sprinklers can successfully cope with an outbreak of fire by "nipping it in the bud" has been abundantly proved, and is fully realised by the insurance companies, who are prepared to insure highly inflammable mills and premises when furnished with sprinkler installations that they would not before accept, and where premises are insured at a very high rate, the insurance companies are prepared to reduce the rate of premium upon the installation of the sprinkler system.

Stop-Back or Reflux Valves—Stop-back valves have been referred to, and their purpose indicated in the first chapter on distribution. It will not therefore be necessary to further explain their use. Fig. 55 is a section of a stop-back with a leather face upon the door, which beats upon a cast-iron face forming part of the casting of the body of the valve. They are also made with gun-metal faces. The gun-metal faced stop-backs, if scraped to a true bearing, are less likely to require after-attention

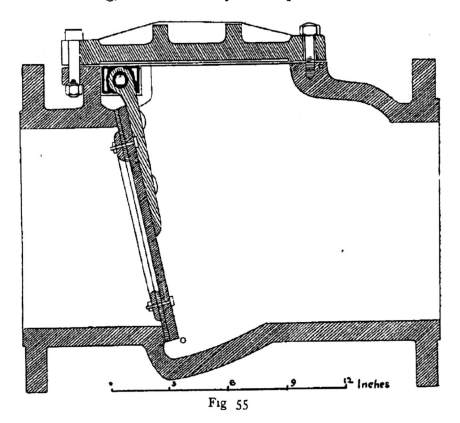

Fig 55

than the leather-faced ones, and for this reason are preferable.

Pressure-Reducing Valves and Apparatus.—Pressure-reducing valves are sometimes necessary, as mentioned in last chapter. In certain hilly districts they are requisite for reducing the pressure in the lower parts.

Fig. 56 is a simple and effective valve for this purpose. Upon the spindle of the valve by which the water passes is fixed a cup leather valve open upon one side to the atmosphere, and against which a certain proportion of the head is expended. The amount by which the pressure is reduced is regulated by the relative area of the valves. There are various forms of pressure-reducing valves, which can be adjusted by a spring or lever arrangement for varying pressures, but where the conditions of pressure do not vary, the form of valve shown

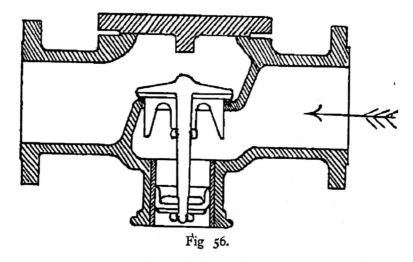

Fig 56.

is sufficient. Where, instead of reducing the pressure by a certain proportion only, the fall on the line of pipe is so great that the whole of the pressure can be taken off, there being sufficient fall for the water to regain the necessary statical head at the lower parts, a break-pressure tank is employed, as shown by Figs. 57 and 58, in section and plan. Its action is self-evident. The water enters tank through a ball-valve which is closed by the float when the water reaches a certain level, and as the water passes away through outlet pipe from tank, the ball-valve comes into action again. The apparatus shown has a by-pass arrangement, and also a wash-out and overflow from tank. The latter is in case the ball-valve leaks at any time.

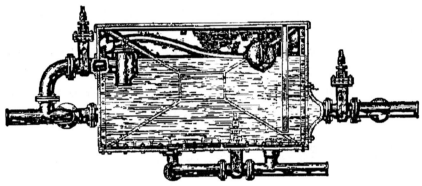

Fig. 57.

Relief-Valves.—Relief-valves are not often necessary except upon pumping mains, where sluice-valves may possibly be shut down by accident against a pumping engine. They are generally regulated by levers and

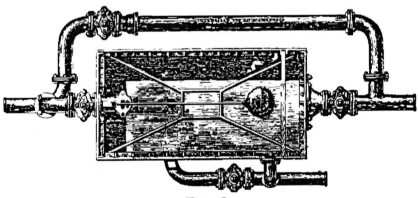

Fig. 58.

weights, which are set to a certain pressure for a safe head upon the mains. If a pressure occurs from any cause in excess of that at which they are set, it overcomes the weight and lever and allows the water to escape, thereby relieving the pressure on the main. An illustration in this case is considered unnecessary, as the valve is, in principle and action, practically identical with the well-known boiler safety-valve.

Self-Closing Valves.—Self-closing valves, or self-acting throttle valves, are for the purpose of shutting off the water in the event of a burst occurring upon a line of main. Examples occur of very large valves of this

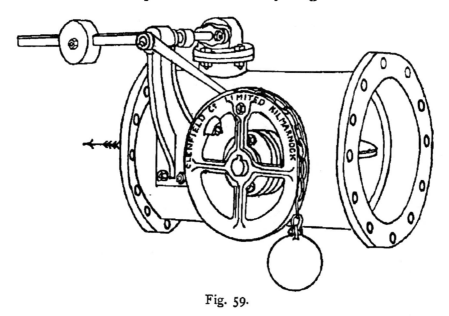

Fig. 59.

description upon the new works before referred to for the supply of Manchester and Liverpool. They are also a very great safeguard upon the leading mains for distribution.

Fig. 59 shows a simple form of such an apparatus. When the velocity of the current exceeds a certain limit (as would be the case in the event of a fracture upon the line of main), a disc which is held by a lever and projects in the water-way is thrown back, thus releasing wheel and weight, and closing the throttle valve. The valve is re-set by hand.   This type is suitable only for placing on the main near its source, and where quick closing will do no damage.   Where the valve is required to close gradually, it is regulated by a cataract arrangement, and the larger sizes are re-set by a pump or by wheel gearing.   Valves of this description can be fitted with electric connections, which make contact and actuate alarm bells when the valves come into action.

Street-Watering Posts.—Figs. 60 and 61 are two forms of street-watering posts. Where the water supply is in the hands of a private company, and a charge has to be made to the road authorities for street-watering, a meter will be fixed between the sluice-valve and the water-post as shown in Fig. 60.

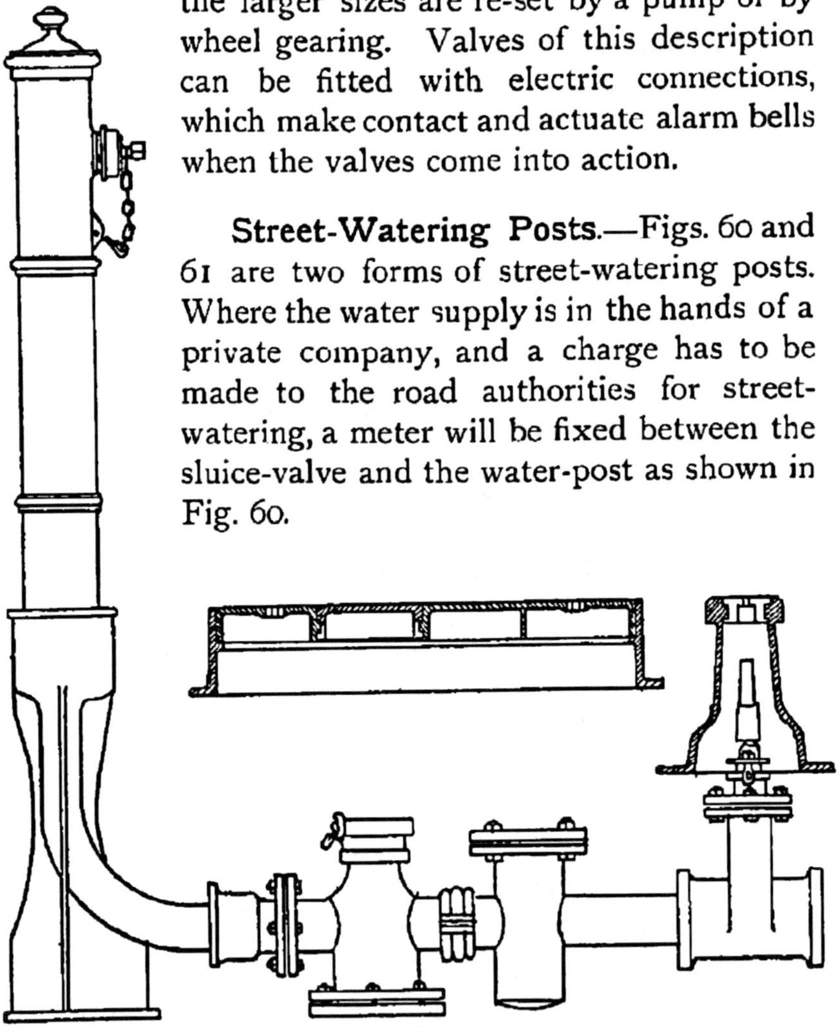

Fig. 60.

With the watering-post shown by Fig. 60, a short length of hose must be carried by the street-watering cart to be attached to the pillar each time the cart is filled for delivering the water into the cart.

On the other hand, with the watering-post shown by Fig. 61, a swan neck is seen which can be left upon the watering-post all the time it is in use for filling cart. It is, however, a very unsightly object to be left standing on water-post, for which reason the other form is very often preferred, although the flexible hose has to be connected each time of filling cart.

The screw-down fire-hydrants, with gun-metal screwed outlets, can be used for street-watering instead of the pillars, but they are not so handy to attach the hose to for filling carts. Moreover, if they were used, the carts might be filled anywhere, which would be apt to be very detrimental to the general supply, because, as before pointed out, the draught for street-watering is a very heavy tax upon the supply, and the positions for the water-pillars require to be very carefully chosen at points

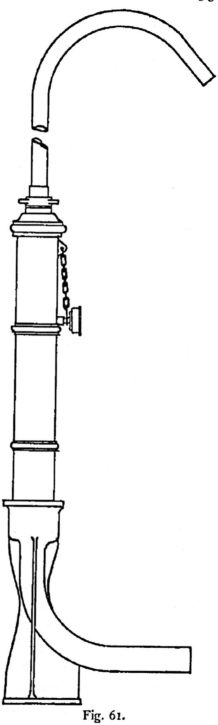

Fig. 61.

where there is plenty of main room to draw upon.

Apparatus for Drilling Trunk Mains and Making Branch Connections to same under Pressure.— Pearson's patent drilling apparatus, for the purpose above described, is made in two forms. The arrangement in general use is shown by Fig. 62.

The action of the apparatus is as follows :—The pipe to be drilled has first secured to it a saddle-piece attached by straps, and making a water-tight joint. To the flange of outlet of saddle-piece a sluice-valve is secured, and a stuffing-box bolted on to same, as shown.

Previous to this having been secured, the drill-spindle has already been passed through the stuffing-box and gland, the crown-cutter, with cutters and central drill, being secured to spindle by a collar pin.

The ratchet is then worked until the central drill has pierced the pipe. The crown-cutters then come into use, and cut out the disc of metal according to the size of hole required.

To the central drill are fitted a pair of small hinged arms or pauls, which fold in while the drill is boring the body of the pipe ; when the pipe is pierced the arms fall out, and the disc of metal cut out by crown-cutters is transfixed on central drill, and so prevented from falling into the pipe.

When the hole is thus formed, the drill with the disc of metal upon it is withdrawn past the sluice-valve, the door of which is then closed.

The closing of the valve having been effected, the stuffing-box and drill and ratchet are removed, when the pipes for which the branch has been formed can be connected and extended to wherever required.

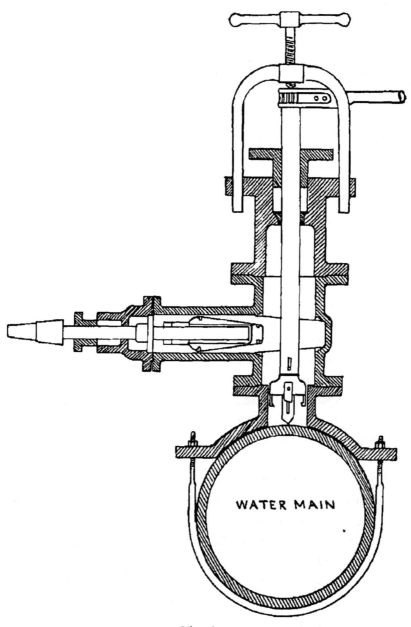

Fig 62.

This apparatus enables branch connections to be made without shutting off the supply and emptying long lengths of pipes.

Besides the avoidance of cutting off the water supply from a district, a further advantage is gained in the saving of water wasted in emptying the pipes. It also does away with the trouble and time spent in re-charging the main.

This apparatus is of great service for making branch connections to trunk mains for supplying water to motors, hoists, and lifts, and for fire supplies, in large public buildings, corn and flour mills, and manufactories, where a supply from a never-failing source is required ; also for supplies for automatic fire appliances, such as the "sprinkler" installations before described, which are daily coming into more general use.

Apparatus for Drilling and Tapping Water Mains and Inserting Ferrules in same under Pressure.— Messrs J Stone & Co's patent Morris's apparatus for the above purpose is shown by Figs. 63, 64, 65, 66, and 67.

This apparatus enables service connections to be made without turning off the water in the mains, and is a great convenience in many cases where the turning off of the water has to be avoided.

Fig. 63 shows the drilling apparatus applied to a main. The action is self-evident, and hardly requires description. It will be seen that the stuffing-box through which the drilling apparatus works is secured to the main by a saddle-piece and chain-strap. The drill is actuated by a ratchet brace, and when the main is drilled through and tapped, the drill and tap are withdrawn by reversing ratchet arrangement.

The slide D (see Fig. 64) is then closed over opening in main, and the upper part of apparatus detached, and

the drill tap removed from socket of spindle. The lower
part of patent ferrule is then attached to spindle, which is
inserted in the stuffing-box arrangement as before, and the
slide D opened, and the lower part of ferrule screwed into

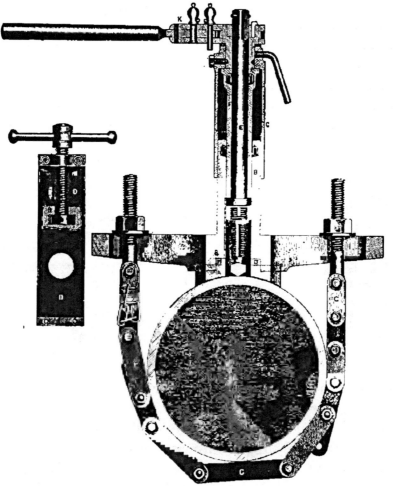

Figs. 63 and 64.

the tapped hole in main. When this is done the whole of
the apparatus is removed, leaving the lower part of
patent ferrule containing the plug-valve in main. The
upper part of the ferrule is then screwed on to part in

main, and the service-pipe connected to outlet of same
in usual way (see Fig. 65), after which the internal plug-
valve is unscrewed by a special key (see Fig. 66) until it
is in the upper part of ferrule, leaving the outlet free for
the passage of water. The cap is then screwed into top
of ferrule, making it perfectly water-tight (see Fig. 67).
This ferrule acts as a stop-cock; if at any time it is
desired to turn the water off, all that has to be done is
to remove cap, and screw down the plug-valve into the
lower part of ferrule. There are other apparatus for
drilling and tapping service connections under pressure,
but Morris's apparatus has been chosen as an excellent

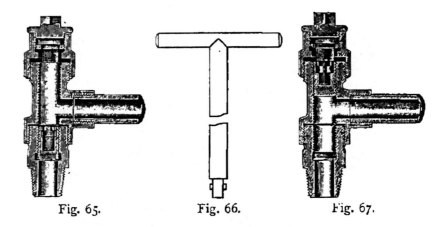

Fig. 65.   Fig. 66.   Fig. 67.

example, and because the writer has had considerable
experience of its satisfactory use.

It is usual upon a system of distribution to divide
up the area of supply into sections, each of which is
liable to be turned off on a certain day for service
connections or repairs, in order to avoid having the
same mains off more than once in a week (except, of
course, where unavoidable in case of accident). The
day upon which each section of distributing area is
liable to be turned off is called the "district day" for
that portion, and new services are only fixed upon it on

that day, and the local plumbers, if they require the water turned off for repairs or alteration, must give notice for the "district day." Even under these restrictions, the turning off of the water is an inconvenience, and where it can be avoided by drilling under pressure, it is a great advantage.

There are also special cases where it is necessary to make ferrule connections to important leading mains, when an apparatus as described for drilling under pressure is indispensable.

Ferrule Connections.—The connections to the dis-

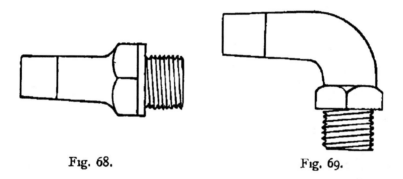

Fig. 68.   Fig. 69.

tributing mains for domestic and small trade supplies, when not connected under pressure, are generally made with the ordinary form of ferrules.

Where the connection is made at the side of the main, the ferrule is of the form shown by Fig. 68, or if the connection is on top of the main, a ferrule with an elbow bend is used, as shown by Fig. 69, these have tinned ends for wiping on the lead pipe.

There are several other forms of ferrules Some have union joints, so that the service can be disconnected at any time at the main by simply unscrewing the cap. These ferrules, for connecting either to the side or on top of the main, are shown by Figs. 70 and 71.

Other ferrules have patent joints for making the connection to the service-pipe without solder.

Very handy forms of ferrule and stop-valve combined are sometimes used. Fig. 72 shows a very good pattern used in Birmingham, known as "Deale's stop-valve ferrule," the invention of the late Mr John Gray.

Service-Pipe.—The service-pipes for domestic supplies and trade purposes, where the diameter is less than 2 inches, are generally lead. Suitable weight pipes for

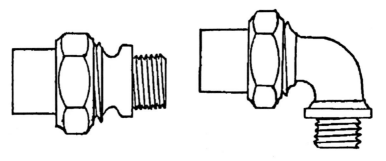

Fig. 70   Fig. 71.

a distributing system such as our example are given in the following table :—

Internal Diameter.	Weight per Yard
inch. $\frac{3}{8}$	lb $5\frac{1}{2}$
$\frac{1}{2}$	7
$\frac{3}{4}$	11
1	15
$1\frac{1}{4}$	19
$1\frac{1}{2}$	24

The waterworks inspectors are usually provided with gauges, with which they can try the internal and external diameter of the pipes laid by the consumers to ascertain if they are of the necessary section for the weights prescribed by the waterworks authorities.

Galvanised wrought-iron pipes and compo' pipes are also sometimes employed for service connections.

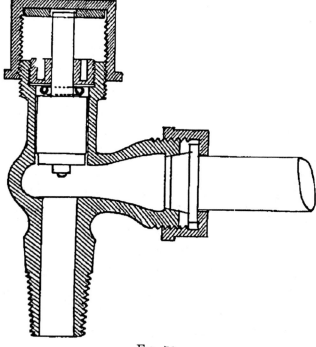

Fig. 72.

WATERWORKS CONSUMERS' FITTINGS.

Coming next to the fittings upon the consumers' services, for trade and domestic supplies :—

Stop-Cocks.—The first apparatus will be the stop-cocks or valves. Every supply, whether by meter or otherwise, should be commanded by a suitable stop-cock or sluice-valve.

I

Plug-Cocks.—Where the supply is by meter, plug-cocks are suitable for the smaller sizes, as they allow a clear way for the flow of the water.

Screw-Down Sluice Door-Cocks—For the larger size meter supplies, the plug-cocks are not advisable, as in closing they arrest the flow of water too suddenly and cause concussion in the mains ; and screw-down sluice door-valves are preferable.

Screw-Down Loose Valve-Cocks. — The well-known Guest & Chrimes' loose valve-cocks, as shown by Fig 73, are universally known, and are very largely employed. They are very efficient and durable. It sometimes happens, however, that in case of stoppage in a service-pipe it is necessary to employ a force-pump to force the obstruction back through the service-pipe, but this cannot be done on account of the

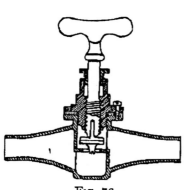

Fig. 73.

loose valve being on its seat when the flow is reversed. To obviate this, they are made, where required, with a pin attachment, so that the loose valve is held up off its seat by the stem of stop-cock when opened.

Diaphragm Stop-Cocks.—Lambert's pattern diaphragm stop-cocks, as shown by Fig 74, are very well known and largely used.

Lord Kelvin's Patent Stop-Cocks are very efficient and durable. It will be unnecessary to describe them here, as the same principle applied to bib-taps will be illustrated and explained under that heading. There are various other patterns of stop-cocks, but it is unnecessary to multiply examples.

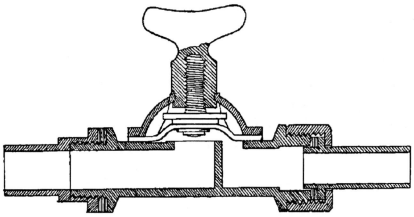

Fig 74.

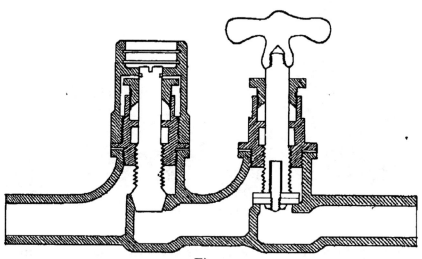

Fig 75.

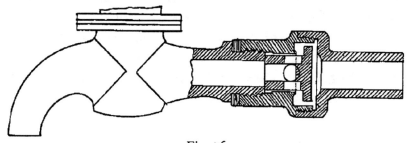

Fig. 76.

Double Stop-Cocks. — Fig. 75 shows Doulton's double regulating valve for trough closets, urinals, fountains, etc. The valve on the right is the same pattern as Fig. 73, before described; but in addition there is a second valve, as shown on the left, which can be permanently set to any rate of flow required for charging trough closets or for the supply of fountains or urinals, whenever the valve on the right is opened.

Stop-Boss. — Fig. 76 shows a form of stop-boss to enable bib-cocks to be removed for repairs without turn-

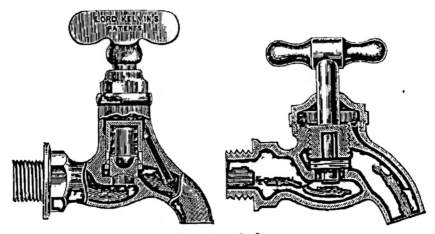

Figs. 77 and 78.

ing off the water. The action is evident from the sketch. When the tap is in place it keeps the stop-boss off its seat, and consequently open. Directly that the tap is unscrewed for repairs it releases stop-boss, and the pressure of water closes same. This appliance is very useful where there is no stop-cock on the domestic supply, but where the service-pipe is commanded by a stop-cock the stop-boss is unnecessary.

Bib-Taps. — There are a great variety of bib-taps.

Some of the oldest types are the Guest & Chrimes' loose valve, and Lambert's diaphragm. It is unnecessary to show illustrations of these, as they are similar in principle to the stop-cocks of corresponding patterns.

Lord Kelvin's patent bib-tap, before referred to, is shown by Fig. 77. It is a very durable fitting. The composite metal valve is not brought to a sudden stop, but is seated gradually, receiving a gradually increasing pressure from the spring applied through the rounded head of the rivet stop. The turning of the spindle revolves valve upon its seat, thereby maintaining a perfect fit and burnish. No packing is used to prevent upward leakage. All water which passes upwards when the tap is opened is drawn off into the bib by the current induced in the eduction tube. This arrangement does away with the necessity for any stuffing-box.

Beck's patent loose valve bib-tap without stuffing-box is shown by Fig. 78. It has the eduction tube, as in Lord Kelvin's tap, which renders a stuffing-box unnecessary; but instead of the metal valve it has a loose valve with leather or indiarubber washer. This is a very good class bib-tap. Beck & Company are also the patentees of a very reliable positive water-meter.

There are a number of other very good types of bib-taps to which it would be impossible to give space.

Self-Closing Bib-Tap. — This description of tap must be of such a character that it will not close with too sudden a jerk to cause concussion. Glenfield patent self-closing tap is a very good type, as shown by Fig. 79. When the button is pressed, the small centre valve opens first, then the main valve opens, and the tap discharges full bore. The spring underneath is simply to carry weight of valve spindle and overcome friction. This tap is fitted with the same arrangement of eduction tube as the last two named, to do away with the necessity of a stuffing-box.

Careless Bib-Tap.—This description of tap has a lever and weight on spindle that falls in case of tap being left partly open, and by means of a quick thread on spindle closes the valve and shuts off the tap.

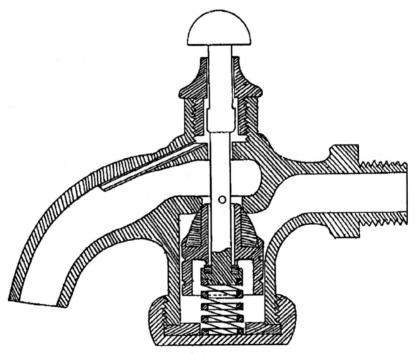

Fig. 79.

Ball-Valves.—Ball-valves are used in connection with W.C service boxes and cisterns. The valve is actuated by an arm or lever, attached to the end of which is a float, generally consisting of a hollow copper ball.

When the water is drawn out of the cistern, the float falls as the level of the water lowers, and opens valve admitting more water. As the water rises in cistern, the arm or lever is raised by the buoyancy of the float,

and shuts the valve when the water has attained a certain
level in the cistern. There are a large number of patterns
of ball-valves. The simplest type of all, and doubtless
for that reason most universally used, is shown by
Fig. 80, in which a solid indiarubber plug closes against
the pressure The only objection to this form of ball-
valve is that it closes against the pressure, and therefore
the passage for the discharge of the water has to be
restricted, otherwise where the pressure is high, it would
necessitate a very large float and long arm or lever to
overcome the pressure against a large valve area, and as
the W.C. cisterns are made of very limited size, this

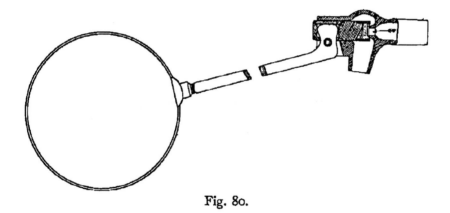

Fig. 80.

would be a serious difficulty. It is, however, a very
efficient ball-valve for general use; and where a cistern
is lodged up under a roof in the peculiarly inaccessible
position often assigned to it by the builder, the more
simple the ball-valve, and therefore less likely it is to get
out of order, the better.

There are many varieties of ball-valves specially constructed to overcome the objection of closing against the
pressure.

Some of the earliest makes are Lambert pattern
equilibrium ball-valves, one type of which is shown by

Fig. 81, the principle of which is self-evident. Wilkes'
patent ball-valve, manufactured by Messrs Guest &
Chrimes, and shown by Fig. 82, is another form of
equilibrium valve, and there are other patterns by various
makers.

Other ball-valves are made to close with the pressure.
They are a great safeguard against leakage, as the pressure helps to keep the valve to its seat. Chorley's patent

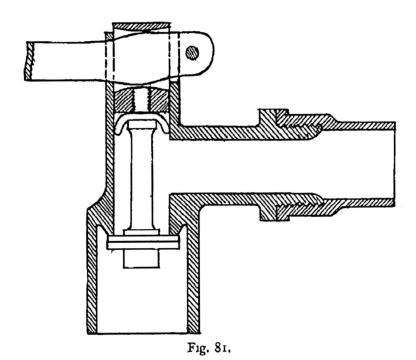

Fig. 81.

safety ball-valve, shown by Fig. 83, is a type of ball-valve
of this description, the valve closing with the pressure.
Hussey's patent ball-valve (Fig. 84) is another pattern
valve that closes with the pressure. A smaller ball and
shorter arm or lever can be used with these valves, as the
buoyancy and leverage are not required to anything like
the same extent as where the valve closes against the
pressure. Care must be taken, however, that the lever

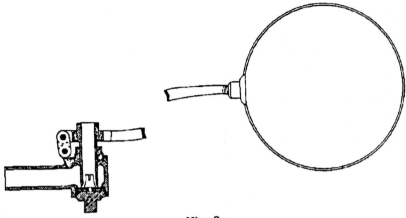

Fig. 82.

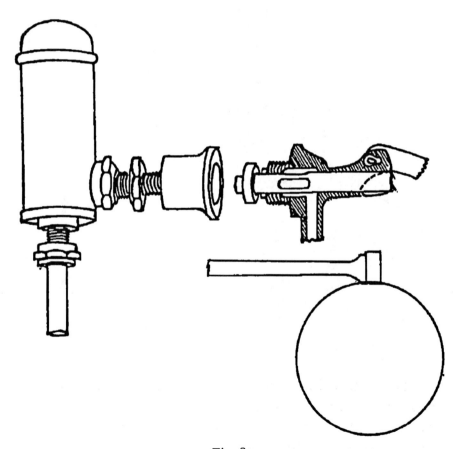

Fig. 83.

is long enough or the ball sufficiently weighted so that
where the pressure of the water is great, acting as it does
in the same direction as that in which the valve closes, it
shall not overcome the weight and leverage, and raise
the float and close valve before the cistern is full.

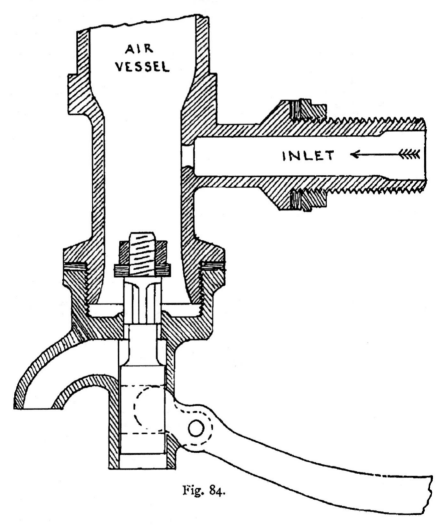

Fig. 84.

Bath and Lavatory Fittings.—It is not necessary
to give any description of the various bath and lavatory
taps and fittings, except to refer to the locking apparatus,
the provision of which, in connection with the bath taps,

being sometimes stipulated by the waterworks authorities to prevent undue waste.

The object of the locking apparatus is to render it impossible to have the supply to the bath and the waste open at the same time.

There are several forms of locking apparatus. Liggat's patent has a loose sleeve upon the waste spindle with two projecting horns, which become fixed when the waste is open, and prevent the hot or cold taps being turned. Shanks' locking apparatus differs somewhat from Liggat's, but is very similar in principle. Tylor's is another form of locking apparatus. It has projecting webs or feathers upon the waste spindle which prevent the hot or cold supplies being turned when the waste is up. Pearson's patent locking apparatus is a very secure locking arrangement, in which two plates, having diagonal slots, are caused to move in a horizontal direction, thereby locking the waste valve spindle when the hot or cold valves are opened, or if the waste is opened, it prevents the movement of the plates, and thereby locks the hot and cold supplies.

Flushing Cisterns for W.C.'s —The service boxes or cisterns for flushing W.C's have latterly engaged the attention of a great number of manufacturers. The object aimed at, as stipulated by the waterworks authorities, is the providing of a sufficient flush of water, generally about 2 or 2½ gallons, with an arrangement to prevent a continuous discharge and waste of water, so that if the handle or " pull up " is held after the regulation quantity is discharged, no more water shall flow until the handle is released and the cistern has had time to refill by means of the ball-valve.

Alternating Valve Cisterns.—Among the earliest

make of cisterns for this purpose was the pattern known as the "73 X," as first manufactured by Messrs Guest & Chrimes (see Fig 85). As an alternating type of service box, this is an admirable pattern. The lower chamber or shoe contains a 2-gallon flush, and the reserve holds about 5 gallons. When the handle is pulled, the alternating valves are actuated, the one on the right closing the communication between the reserve and the flushing chamber, and the centre valve being opened to allow the discharge of the 2-gallon flush.

There are several other alternating valve cisterns, but none of a simpler or better design than the "73 X."

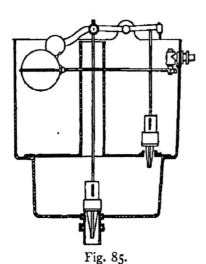

Fig. 85.

Bell's valves, shown by Fig. 86, accomplish the same purpose as the alternating valves. A hollow tube, as shown, passes through a metal bush in the partition separating the flushing chamber from the reserve tank. When the valves are at rest, the weighted valve attached to the stem at bottom of hollow tube is closed, and water can pass freely from the reserve to the flushing chamber by means of the double row of orifices in the hollow tube. By pulling the handle and chain attached to lever, the lower valve is lifted off its seat, but not until the hollow spindle is raised, so that the lower row of orifices are within the metal bush, and the flow of water between the reserve and flushing chamber thereby practically stopped. The loose valve arrangement for this purpose is an improvement upon the original "Bell's valve," and prevents the possibility of the water flowing into and out

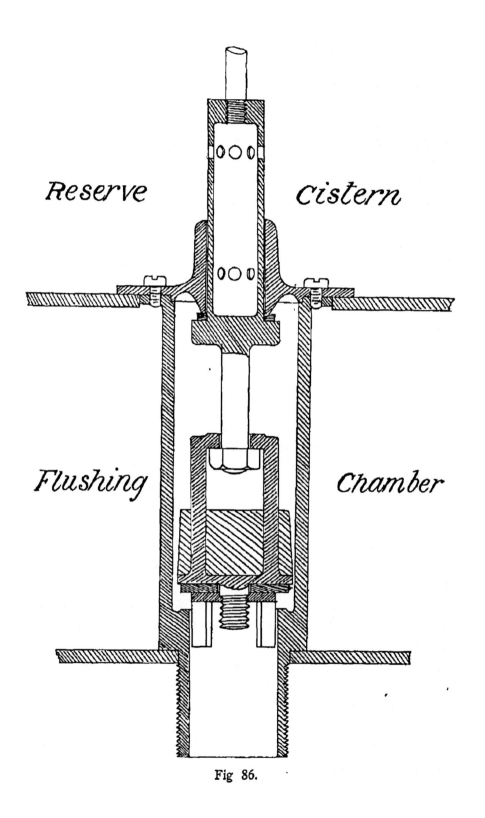

Reserve   Cistern

Flushing   Chamber

Fig 86.

of the reserve chamber at the same time　When the hollow spindle is fully raised, as shown in Fig. 86, the upper valve seating entirely seals the communication between the reserve and the flushing chamber, and the lower valve is then full open, allowing a free discharge from the flushing chamber

Syphon Cisterns.—Of late years syphon cisterns have come greatly into vogue, and are preferred by many on account of their simplicity of action, and the absence of working parts　Moreover, they have another feature that commends itself to some, namely, that even if the handle is released before the flush is complete, the entire contents of the cistern will be discharged, the syphon action having once started.

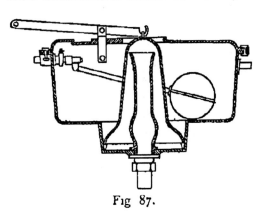

Fig 87.

Doubtless a well-designed syphon cistern is very satisfactory, but great care should be exercised in the selection of a suitable pattern to ensure a proper flush, and run no risk of the syphon action being uncertain, and the cistern should be so designed that the syphon action is effectually broken when the proper flush is discharged.　Broadly speaking, there are two classes of syphon cistern　In the first, the action is started by displacement, and in the second, by the lifting action generally of a disc arrangement.

1. *By Displacement.*—These have a bell or bonnet arrangement, as shown by Shanks' "Levern" pattern (Fig. 87).　When the bonnet is lifted, no action takes place

until it is released, when in lowering it displaces a certain quantity of water, and, owing to its bell-shaped section, the displacement by the larger area of the bottom causes sufficient overflow in the smaller upper area of bonnet over the down leg of syphon to start the action, and discharge the contents of the cistern. This type of cistern, if properly designed, is very certain in its action, and extremely simple, and may be very economically made.

2. *By Lifting Action of Disc Arrangement.*—This type of cistern is made in many forms. Winn's " New

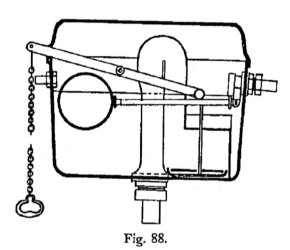

Fig. 88.

River " cistern, shown by Fig. 88, is a very good example. The pulling of the handle and chain moves the lever in the usual manner, raising the stem and disc in the cylinder shown on the right hand side, which is connected by the bent neck with the down leg of syphon. The lifting of disc raises the water over the neck of syphon, starting the action which continues until the contents of cistern are discharged. In this type of cistern the action commences at once with the raising of disc, and in this respect it differs from the bonnet type.

It will be seen that the disc is not in one piece. The

fixed portion attached to stem fits approximately the diameter of cylinder which is necessary to lift the water and start syphon action. But there is also a loose disc which rests on top of the fixed one, and is very thin and light, so that when the discharge of water is once started, it offers very little opposition to the uprush and rises off the fixed disc, in which there are a series of holes to allow the contents of cistern to pass through freely. There are a variety of patterns of syphon cistern upon the disc principle, many of them of excellent design. In some a hinged flap replaces the loose disc, others have a horizontal or radial motion instead of the vertical action.

In all syphon cisterns it is desirable that the top of the syphon should be above the top of cistern to prevent any likelihood of a continuous action occurring, and for the same reason there should be plenty of clearance at the bottom of cylinder, so as to break the syphon action when the contents of cistern is discharged or nearly so.

Attention should be paid to the size and discharging capacity of ball-valve supply cistern, and to the circumstances under which the cistern is supplied with water. If the supply is direct and under a high pressure, a $\frac{3}{8}$-inch ball-valve is large enough, as a $\frac{1}{2}$-inch ball-valve would allow the water to enter cistern so fast that it would be likely to unduly prolong the flush. On the other hand, where there is an indirect supply to syphon cistern from an adjoining tank, the ball-valve should be $\frac{1}{2}$ inch full way, or the syphon cistern will be an excessive time in refilling, with only a few feet head of water on ball-valve.

A drawback to the syphon cisterns has hitherto been that they have no reserve flush should the water be unavoidably off for some time, except they are supplied from a separate reserve cistern; but the writer understands that syphon cisterns are being introduced with a reserve flush, which will meet this objection where it is raised. On the other hand, the syphon cisterns are simple and cleanly, and have helped towards the abandonment of the old hopper pan W.C.'s.

The modern tendency is to have all the sanitary arrangements as open and above-board as possible. This is as it should be, and the beautiful glazed and enamelled cisterns and pans and modern lavatory fittings, are a great advance on the old style.

The down pipe from the service box to the pan should be of ample size to give an unrestricted flush, as a rapid flush with a moderate amount of water is far more effectual than a slow flush with a much larger quantity. In no case should a down pipe of less than $1\frac{1}{4}$ inches in internal diameter be allowed.

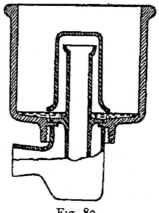

Fig. 89.

Flushing Cisterns for Urinals.—Service boxes or cisterns are also used for flushing urinal basins. They may be of either the alternating valve type or syphon action. The quantity discharged at each flush is generally from 1 to $1\frac{1}{4}$ gallons, or about half that of the W.C. service boxes.

Self-Acting Flushing Tanks for Troughs, Closets, Urinals, etc.—Large self-acting syphon flushing cisterns are used for flushing ranges of trough closets, urinals, sewage chambers, etc Doulton's patent automatic flush tank is one of this type, as shown by Fig. 89. The cistern is so simple that it needs very little description , a double stop-cock, as before described, supplies water to the flush tank at a certain rate as required, so that at regular inter-

K

vals the water rises in flush tank to the height necessary to start syphon action, when the whole of the contents of the flush tank is discharged. The small lower chamber forms a trap to seal the lower end of the syphon pipe.

SURFACE BOXES FOR VALVES, HYDRANTS, ETC.

Surface boxes in great varieties are made for sluice-valves, hydrants, air-escapes, meters, stop-cocks, etc. Patterns suitable for almost every possible requirement may be referred to in the illustrated catalogues of the leading hydraulic makers, so that it is only a matter of judgment and common-sense to select the kinds best fitted for the conditions that may arise. It would be quite superfluous to give a series of illustrations here, when so many excellent patterns may be readily referred to. A few hints will be all that is necessary for guidance in their selection. First as to :—

Surface Boxes for Sluice-Valves.—Those for the sluice-valves on the distributing mains in the roadways may be of the type shown by Fig. 90, with a round top, and cover slightly tapered with chequered surface. It might be said here that all surface-box covers, where of cast-iron, should have properly chequered surfaces to prevent horse or pedestrian slipping. There should be a hole in the cover, as shown, for loosening and drawing same with the turncock's tools. The cover need not be more than about $3\frac{1}{2}$ inches in diameter to allow of an opening large enough to insert the key for opening and closing valve, and so as not to be large enough for a horse to get his hoof in, in case of the cover being missing, except for the large sized valves, which are worked by bigger keys, and therefore require larger openings and covers. The body of the surface box or cock casing, as it is generally termed, should be conical, with a stout flange at bottom to rest on the brickwork walling built up around valve. It is well to have openings in the sides of casings as shown to clear the stuffing-boxes of valves.

Where the casings are made from 12 to 18 inches deep of the pattern shown, they require less walling. Some patterns are made much shallower, and a separate protecting tube is fixed over stuffing-box.

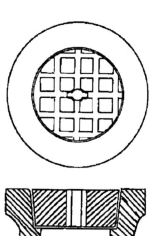

There are various kinds of locking and hinged lids that can be satisfactorily used where the boxes are situated in the foot pavements, but for use in the roadways, where the covers are subjected to heavy traffic, and to moisture of a peculiarly corroding nature, they are none of them altogether satisfactory. The locking arrangement is liable to stick fast, and the shoulders of the hinged covers to break off.

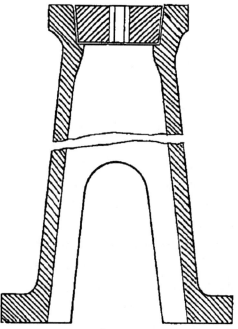

Fig. 90.

The outcome of experience is to have neither the locking nor hinged lid arrangement. The covers should be all interchangeable, so that they can be easily replaced if missing, and be made slightly tapered with a full $\frac{1}{16}$-inch clearance all round, and there will seldom be any difficulty in loosening and withdrawing them. It is well to drive a small piece of wood in the holes in covers when they are fixed, to prevent the urchins pulling them up. Even then they will be occasionally missing, but by arrangement with the police they will be immediately reported and replaced.

For the casings of important valves on leading mains, or where a lot of valves are close together, to avoid confusion it is well to have indicating plates upon the under sides of covers, describing what the valves are. The plates are best made in solid brass, with raised letters. Where indicating plates are fixed, larger covers, of about 5 inches in diameter, are required, which should be securely attached to inside of bodies of casings with loose chains, so that the covers can be lifted, but not changed.

Surface Boxes for Hydrants.—These are rectangular in shape, and require to be large enough to fix the stand-pipe and work the valve-key. Where they are to be situated in the roadway they must not be less than about 9 inches deep, for the bottom flange to be below the wood or stone setts, and the box and cover must be stout enough to withstand the road traffic.

Where situated in the footways, the boxes need not be so stout, and about 5 or 6 inches will be deep enough in order that the bottom flanges may be below the flag-stones or other paving. The covers should be chained.

Surface Boxes for Meters.—The surface boxes for meters should be of ample size to enable the meter registers to be read, and to admit of the meters being exchanged when necessary, without having to open the ground. The meters should be fixed so that the boxes are not in the roads or hauling ways where they are for large size meters. The covers should preferably be iron frames with stone covers let in ; and in two halves when for extra large size boxes for 3-inch meters and upwards.

It is never advisable to have very large iron covers, as even when in the pavement they are a source of danger, and in the roadway so much so, that the street authorities are unlikely to sanction them. Where a large box has to be in the roadway, the most suitable type is the iron frame with hardwood blocks inserted.

Large covers in the roadway should have a special tight bearing surface to exclude wet and dirt. This is absolutely essential where there is any indicating gear in the chamber. Special boxes are made by Messrs Blakeborough and other hydraulic firms, with a V-shaped projection around the under side of edge of cover which rests upon a lead seating in rim of box making a tight joint, and such covers should have box castings on opposite sides of cover for the holes in which keys are to be inserted for lifting, as the holes must not go right through cover, because of the necessity for the exclusion of wet and dirt.

Surface Boxes for Stop-Cocks.—These, where the stop-cocks are in the roadway, will be very similar to the smaller valve surface boxes, but where in the foot-ways they may be shallower and of lighter make.

All surface boxes should be coated with Dr Angus Smith's patent composition, and where thought necessary, distinguishing letters can be cast upon them.

Walling Up Valves, Hydrants, etc.—All sluice-valves, hydrants, meters, stop-cocks, etc., should be care-fully walled up with hard stock bricks, properly and evenly bedded and finished to a flat surface to take the bottom flange of surface box, otherwise the valves and meters will be choked up with dirt falling in from the sides ; and especial care should be taken in having the walling properly and securely fixed for the hydrants, as if it bulges into the chamber, so that the stand-pipes cannot be immediately fixed in case of fire, serious trouble is likely to arise. Although the pits require to be well walled up, the bottoms must not be rendered water-tight, as there would then be trouble with storm-water remaining in the pits, or in the case of the fire-hydrants after flushing.

Pitching around Surface Boxes.—All surface boxes in steined roads, or gravel, or such-like surfaces, should be pitched round, otherwise the surface is liable to be worn or washed away around them until they become a source of danger to traffic.

Indicating Plates for Fire-Hydrants.—Indicating plates require to be fixed in a conspicuous position upon the walls or houses opposite to where the hydrants are situated, with enamelled or painted or raised metal letters, and figures indicating the distance of the hydrants from the wall.

Pipe-Laying Tools, Turncocks, Keys, and Sundry Waterworks Requisites

If the waterworks authorities open the ground themselves, they require the usual picks and shovels, and other equipments for opening and making good ground ; but this part of the work is very often let to contractors, and it is not thought necessary to enter here into particulars of trench-work and excavating.

Pipe-Laying.—This is nearly always done by the

waterworks authorities, as it requires great care and experience. Particulars have already been given of the jointing. There are a variety of apparatus required—such as shear-legs for hoisting and lowering pipes, pipe carriages, fire-grates, lead pots and ladles, hammers and chisels, pipe-laying tools, ratchet braces, drills, pipe-cutters, etc. They may be found catalogued and illustrated in the trade publications of the manufacturers who lay themselves out for this class of work.

Turncocks and Meter-Takers' Keys.—Sets of keys and bars are made to suit the various requirements for opening the valves and hydrants, and lifting the surface-box covers. These again are to be found in the illustrated catalogues, and need no special description here.

Plumbers' Tools.—The plumbing tools are of the usual kind, forming part of a plumber's stock-in-trade.

Sundry Requisites.—It would be useless to attempt to enumerate all the requisites necessary for the equipment of a system of distribution, as it embraces most trades, and articles as unlike as an engineer's taps and dies, and a turncock's uniform and badge.

Where the undertaking is a large one, many trades are represented on the staff, and workshops required for the principal branches, such as engineers, blacksmiths, carpenters, and plumbers; but for a small system of distribution it is generally more convenient to employ private tradesmen and contractors for much of the work arising, who find their own plant. But the connection of services and all alterations and repairs to the distributing pipes as well as the pipe-laying should be done by the waterworks authorities' own workmen.

It has been impossible to describe all the waterworks fittings. Many specialities, such as pillar and wall fountains, frost-valves, and minor matters and incidentals, have had to be omitted, but the essential fittings, pipes, valves, etc., have, it is thought, been sufficiently dealt with to enable the reader to form a very fair idea of the principal necessities that come under the heading of this chapter for a system of waterworks distribution, and it is only a matter of detail in actual practice to supplement what is here described, by such additions as may be found necessary when the occasions arise.

CHAPTER V.

*METERS AND MEASUREMENT OF WATER, AND
REGULATING AND RECORDING APPARATUS.*

THE apparatus coming under the heading of this chapter
includes the trade and domestic meters, which are essen-
tially waterworks fittings for distribution, and in that
respect are entitled to a place in the preceding chapter.
It was thought advisable, however, to reserve the description of them for a separate chapter, as they are
better grouped with the other apparatus of a kindred
nature for the measurement of water, and with the regulating and recording apparatus incidental to a system
of distribution.

Meters and Measurement of Water.—Meters for
measuring water under pressure may be positive or
inferential.

Trade and Domestic Meters will be first considered.

Positive Meters.—Positive meters measure the actual
quantity of water passing, and are generally single or
double or three-cylinder meters. The great difficulty
with positive meters is to alternate the flow of the water,
and measure the actual quantity passing with certainty,
and avoid leakage of water slipping by, and at the same
time to reduce the friction to a minimum, so that no
sensible resistance may be offered to the passage of the

water to retard its velocity and reduce the head or pressure.

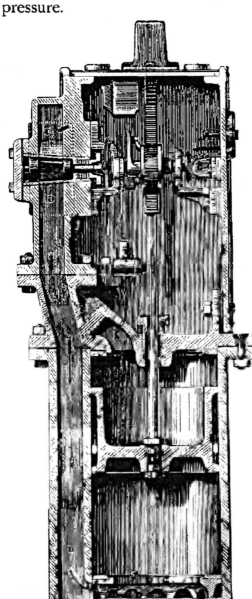

Fig. 91.

It is a very difficult matter to fulfil these requirements satisfactorily, and at the same time to produce a meter at a reasonable cost and of convenient size. There are, however, several positive meters that work reliably. A comparison of their relative merits would not, it is thought, be advisable.

It is proposed to briefly describe one only, and that without prejudice. The example chosen has been fixed upon because it is the positive meter with which the author was first acquainted, and is, it is believed by him, one of the very earliest introduced.

Fig. 91 is a section of the meter known as Kennedy's patent water-meter. The measuring cylinder forms the base of the meter, and is fitted with a piston made to

move water-tight, and almost free from friction, by means
of an indiarubber ring between the surface of the piston
and the cylinder. The piston-rod, after passing through
a stuffing-box in cylinder cover, is attached to a rack
which gears into a pinion fixed on a shaft that actuates
the indexing and reversing gear.   A weighted lever,
shown in a vertical position, is struck by a projecting

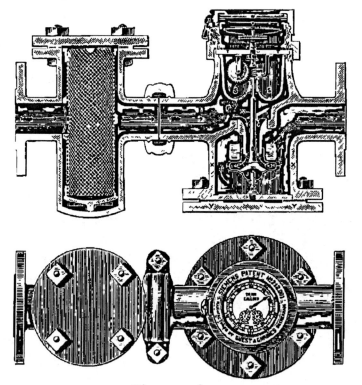

Figs. 92 and 93.

arm on rack as the piston and rack rises and falls, and is
caused to fall alternately on each arm of a duplex lever,
which moves the cock-key and directs the water either
above or below the piston and to the outlet ports.   The
movement of the indexing gear gives a reading upon
the dial or counter of the number of gallons passing the
meter.   Other well-known positive meters are Tylor's

duplex meter, Kent's absolute, Beck's imperial, Frost's Manchester, and the American Worthington meter.

Inferential Meters —The usual form of inferential meters for trade and domestic purposes are those of the rotary type. A standard example of these is the Siemens & Adamson's water-meter. This meter, originally introduced into this country by Messrs Guest & Chrimes in 1854, and the Kennedy positive meter, were, I believe, the earliest meters in use in this country. Figs. 92, 93, and 94 are section and plan of the meter, and enlargement of measuring drum for a 2-inch diameter Siemens meter.

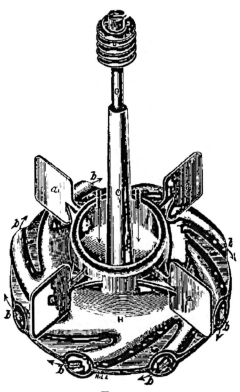

Fig 94

The meter is constructed upon the well-known turbine principle or Barker's mill. The measuring medium consists of a drum working on an upright spindle. The water is conveyed by the conducting tube into the centre of the drum, and allowed to escape at three or more apertures on the periphery of same, giving to it a rotary motion. At each revolution of the drum a certain quantity of water is delivered, which is registered upon a dial by an indexing gear of wheels and pinions.

This meter is made and adjusted with extreme care,

and is exceedingly satisfactory in its working, registering under varying conditions with a very small percentage of error.

The approximate delivery of the Siemens meter in gallons per hour is given by Messrs Guest & Chrimes in the following table. The lesser quantity is based upon 50 feet, and the greater upon 150 feet head :—

⅜ inch will deliver from			150 to	250	gallons per hour.	
½ ,,	,,	,,	300 ,,	500	,,	,,
¾ ,,	,,	,,	600 ,,	1,000	,,	,,
1 ,,	,,	,,	1,500 ,,	2,500	,,	,,
1¼ ,,	,,	,,	2,200 ,,	3,800	,,	,,
1½ ,,	,,	,,	3,000 ,,	5,000	,,	,,
2 ,,	,,	,,	4,000 ,,	7,000	,,	,,
2½ ,,	,,	,,	6,000 ,,	10,000	,,	,,
3 ,,	,,	,,	8,300 ,,	14,000	,,	,,
4 ,,	,,	,,	13,400 ,,	23,000	,,	,,
5 ,,	,,	,,	18,500 ,,	32,000	,,	,,
6 ,,	,,	,,	27,000 ,,	46,000	,,	,,
8 ,,	,,	,,	45,000 ,,	77,000	,,	,,
10 ,,	,,	,,	70 000 ,,	120,000	,,	,,
12 ,,	,,	,,	90,000 ,,	154,000	,,	,,

Another form of Siemens inferential meter, chiefly used abroad, is of the fan type.

Tylor's is another well-known inferential meter of the fan type.

Other forms of meters for trade and domestic use are the volume or capacity meters, chiefly manufactured and used in the United States. Their merit appears to be simplicity and small size and lightness

There are also low-pressure meters, but they are of course unsuitable for the delivery of a supply under pressure.

A very able article has lately appeared in *Engineering*,* by Mr William Schonheyder, entitled "Water

---

* *Engineering*, 2nd and 9th February 1900.

Meters of the Present Day, with Special Reference to Small Flows and Waste in Dribbles," being a copy of a paper read before the Institution of Mechanical Engineers, which can be strongly recommended for careful perusal by those interested in the question of meter supply.

Waste Water-Meters —The Deacon waste water-meter, invented by Mr Geo. F. Deacon, and in general use for the detection and prevention of waste upon distributing systems, has been mentioned in previous chapters, and its application for the prevention of waste described, and the reader was referred to a paper on the subject.

It will be sufficient here to give an illustration and brief description of the meter itself. Fig. 95 shows its form and action clearly. Within a casting, socketed upon line of main, is fitted a gun-metal tapered tube, through which the water passes, as shown by the arrows Guided vertically within this tube is a gun-metal disc, of such size as to fit the smaller end of the tapered tube. From the upper end of the stem of disc a fine wire passes through a packed gland to a small carriage guided vertically, and carrying a pencil. From the carriage a cord passes over a pulley to a counterbalance weight, whose tendency is to keep the disc at the top of tapered tube. The diagram paper is carried upon a drum, which is caused to revolve by clockwork once in twenty-four hours, or by a special arrangement of gearing it may be made to revolve once in six hours for night-inspection purposes.

When water is passing through the main the disc is forced downwards into the larger area, to an extent proportionate to the quantity of water passing, and the pencil is at the same time carried to a corresponding

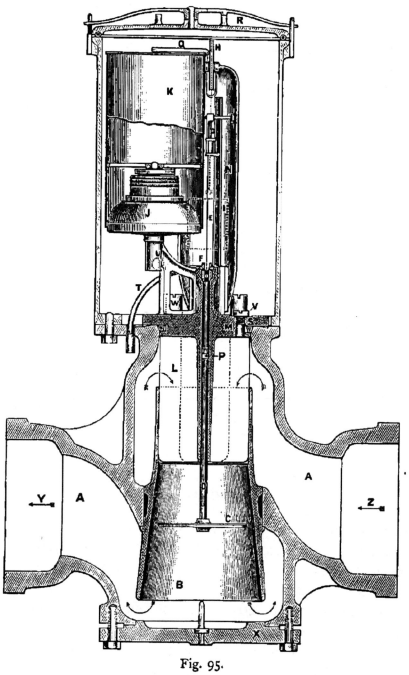

Fig. 95.

point on the diagram paper. The latter is ruled horizontally for gallons per hour, while the pencil moving
vertically records the quantity passing   The drum and
paper revolving cause the quantity to be recorded at the
right time.

The best arrangement for fixing the waste water-
meter is upon a branch pipe, as shown by Fig. 96, commanded by sluice-valves A and B, which can be shut at
any time for the removal or repair of meter, and during

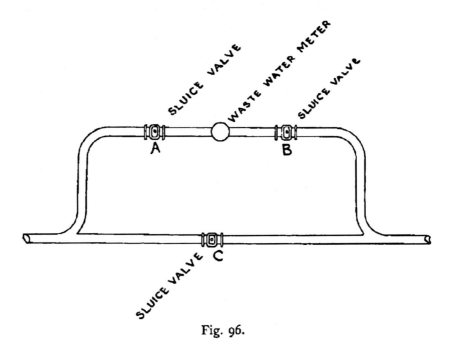

Fig. 96.

such period the by-pass valve C will be opened for the
passage of the water; or where it is not thought desirable to have the flow running constantly through the
waste water-meter, the valve C will be kept open, and
the valves A and B closed, except when the periodical
inspection takes place, when the clock will be fixed, and
the meter set in action and diagram attached, and the
valves A and B opened and C closed.

Venturi Meter for Measurement of Water under Pressure by Velocity.—This meter is designed for the measurement of large volumes of water. It is patented by Mr Clemens Herschel, an American, and manufactured in this country by Mr George Kent, of High Holborn, who is also the patentee and maker of positive rotary meters for trade and domestic purposes, reciprocating piston meters, etc.

A paper was read upon the Venturi meter before the British Association of Waterworks Engineers by Mr Kent, at their London meeting, in July 1897, from which some extracts will be given.

The purpose for which this meter is specially intended is to measure the total volume of water being delivered by the trunk main to a system of distribution, and it is therefore entitled to some description in this treatise The instrument measures water flowing under pressure in mains without any obstruction to the pipe lines or any moving parts in contact with the flowing water.

Measurement is obtained by aid of the Venturi law, that water flowing through a pipe of diminishing area loses lateral pressure as it gains in velocity, so that at the throat of the Venturi tube (see Fig. 97 *) which unites two truncated cones, it is only a question, within a certain limit of static pressure, of obtaining a sufficiently high speed in order to entirely lose all pressure To illustrate the principle, supposing three vertical glass tubes connected to the Venturi tube—one at the inlet, one at the throat, and one at the outlet—and water flowing at a certain velocity, there would be a depression of level in the tube at the throat, but the pressure or level would be almost entirely regained at the down-stream end. The difference of pressure between the up-stream and throat is termed " Venturi head."

---

* See Diagram No. 18, facing page 134.

The Venturi meter consists of two parts, the tube (see Fig. 97*), and the recorder or register (see Fig. 98).

The tube forms part of the ordinary pipe-line. The relation of the area of the throat to the main is entirely governed by the requirements as to maximum and minimum registration. The exterior of the tube is provided at the throat and up-stream end with annular pressure chambers. These communicate with the tube by means of small holes. Two small tubes convey the pressure to the recording apparatus. The recording instrument is fitted with a diagram arrangement showing the rate of flow, and a counter which gives the total quantity passed. It is evident that, with a difference of pressure (Venturi head) between the throat and the up-stream having a constant relation to the discharge from the tube, it is only necessary to multiply the square root of this pressure by the ascertained coefficient and by time in order to obtain the total quantity passed.

The register consists, broadly speaking, of two parts. First, a mercurial U-tube, which brings in the element of the Venturi head; and secondly, of the clockwork and gear, which supplies the element of time. The connection between the pressure and time is established by means of floats resting on the mercury in the U-tube.

In the combined instrument, shown by Fig. 98, we have diagrams giving the rate of flow, and a counter showing the total quantity passed, and both legs of the U-tube are used. The floats carry light racks gearing into pinions, which convey the motion to small pulleys, from which wires pass to the clockwork mechanism, the one on the left to the diagram recorder, and the one on the right to the counter.

That portion of the apparatus belonging to the

---

* On Diagram No. 18, facing this page.

PROJECTION OF SURFACE OF INTEGRATING DRUM

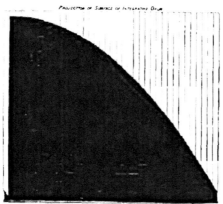

Fig. 99.

UP-STREAM PRESSURE PIPE
TO MANOMETER

THROAT PRESSURE PIPE
TO MANOMETER

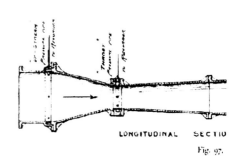

LONGITUDINAL SECTION

Fig. 97.

Pressure Pipe from Up Stream to Piston Tube

Pipe from Throat to Piston Tube

NOTE TO FIG. 98. —The Recording Instrument as now made is modified by the simplification of several details, but the general principle is as illustrated.

Fig. 98.

diagram is so similar to other recording instruments that it requires no special description. It may be fitted either with daily or weekly diagrams, and is ruled with horizontal lines showing the rate of flow, and with vertical lines giving the hours and days.

The counter mechanism is more complicated. In order to comply with the hydraulic law, which makes the quantity discharged through a pipe vary directly as the square root of the head, it is necessary to square root the Venturi head before multiplying it by time to obtain the total quantity passed. That is done in this way :—The integrating drum is constantly revolving so many times an hour. Its surface has two planes, one of the full diameter of the drum, the other of a reduced diameter. The drum is represented on diagram (see Fig. 99) as having been rolled out. The line which separates one portion from another is a square root curve. When the small carriage, the height of which is controlled by the Venturi head, is in contact with the recessed portion, communication is established by means of the spur wheel and pinion with the counter, and registration takes place. When the carriage is in contact with the raised portion of drum, the pinion is held out of gear, and no registration occurs. If no water is passing, the carriage would be at top of drum as shown, on the edge of, but not in, the recess. If, on the other hand, water were passing at full speed, the Venturi head would be at its maximum, the carriage would be at the bottom of the drum and in contact with the recessed portion, and consequently registering the whole time. Registration at any intermediate spot must be in proportion to the square root of the head. For instance, if we imagine the height of drum divided vertically into 4, the registration at 4 would be twice that at 1, the square root of 4 being 2 and 1.1, the horizontal travel at 1 being exactly half that at

4, and at any point it is proportionate to the square root.

Diagram No 19 is a sample diagram taken from a large Venturi meter.

The Venturi meter is well described by Mr J. T. Rodda in his "Notes on Water Supply." To quote from his description : " It enables large bodies of water to be measured easily and accurately.   It determines the leakage of pumps, mains, or reservoirs, and offers to waterworks a means of determining accurately, at little cost, the total quantity of water drawn and the quantity used."

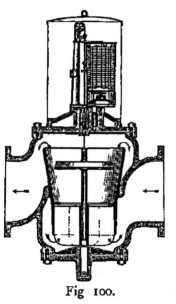

Fig 100.

The register may be placed in any convenient position within 1,000 feet of the tube, and there may also be an electrical device by which the record may be carried any distance from the meter to the engineer's office.

The Venturi meter has been approved and its adoption recommended by Messrs Hawkesley & Mansergh, and other leading engineers.

Large Differentiating Water-Meter for Measurement by Displacement (Deacon's Patent).—This meter is of the same type as the Deacon waste water-meter, but specially constructed for the purpose of measuring large volumes of water issuing from reservoirs in trunk mains under pressure.   The conical tube, in which the water acts upon disc by displacement, is arranged the reverse way to that of the waste water-meter (see Fig. 100).   It is designed so that none of the parts upon which the

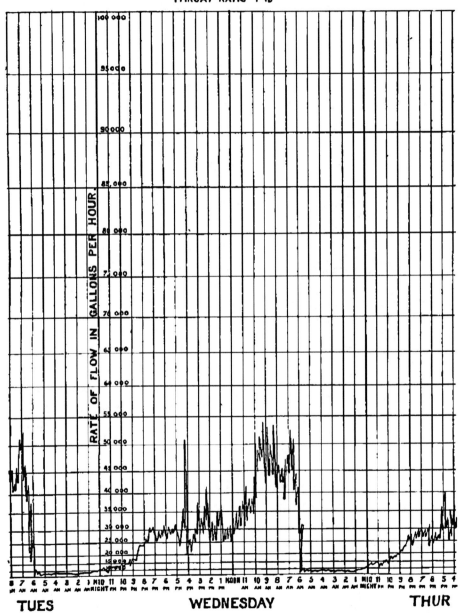

18ᴵᴺ "VENTURI" WATER METER.
THROAT RATIO 1 15

TUES   WEDNESDAY   THUR

gauging depends are in rubbing contact with other surfaces, so that it can continue in work for a very long time without any change in the accuracy of the records.

As usually made, they are actuated by an eight-day clock, and the diagram lasts a week.

Slide-Rule for the Measurement of the Flow of Water in Pipes —Under the title of "Measurement of Water," a slide-rule designed by Mr A. S. Crane, of Brooklyn, and introduced into this country by Mr A. Wollheim, A.M.I C.E., of Leadenhall House, E C., is deserving of mention.

By its use the discharges of pipes or sewers, of different sizes and for various gradients, are obtained very readily.

The slopes or gradients are shown on the lowest scale of rule ; above this on slide are different sizes of pipes or sewers. The graduations of the rule are based on Kutter's formula. Two lines have been engraved on slide for each size of pipe, the pair being connected by a sloping line. The longer of the vertical lines corresponds to a coefficient of roughness of .013, and the shorter to .015.

The upper scale on slide is marked with an arrow, against which the discharge is read on the top scale of rule. In the case of the pipe sewers or conduits running partly full, the upper scale on slide is also marked by arrows, opposite which the discharge can be read when either one-third or two-thirds full. This slide-rule can be graduated to suit a variety of requirements, and is a great saving in labour where discharges have to be frequently calculated.

Measurement of Water when not under Pressure by Gauge Weirs.—The measurement of the quantity of water supplied to a system of distribution where the supply is by gravitation has until lately generally been by means of gauge weirs, the quantity being ascertained and regulated by the depth of flow measured over the weirs.   The weirs are generally situated in a gauge tank at the outlet from the store reservoirs, and a certain depth of flow, regulated by sluices, is allowed, according to the requirements to be met, it being more convenient to measure the quantity out from the store reservoirs than after it has reached the service reservoirs for distribution, because a regular amount can be supplied from store to the service reservoir for the day's supply, which will be delivered from the service reservoir at a variable rate, according to the draught by day and night on the leading mains to the distributing system for the low-level zone, plus the quantity pumped for the high-service supply, the service reservoir acting as a " balance reservoir," as it is sometimes termed—that is, balancing the supply over the twenty-four hours, by storing water at such times as the draught is less than the average amount sent in for the day's supply, and being drawn upon when the draught exceeds the average in the day-time.   Therefore, although the gauge weirs may be situated at the store reservoirs, more or less remote from the district to be supplied, they are directly related to the question of distribution, as by their means the supply of water to the distributing system is regulated ; and even where a Venturi meter is fixed upon the trunk main to measure the total volume of water under pressure, a gauge weir is generally also placed at the point where the supply issues from the store reservoirs.

The gauge weirs may be either rectangular or V-shaped notch weirs or submerged openings.   Various formulæ, arrived at by experiment, are employed for calculating the quantity for any depth of flow for the various forms of weirs.

For the V notch weir the following formula is employed :—

$Q = .305 \ (H \frac{5}{2})$.
Where Q = cubic feet per minute.
   H = height of water in inches from vertex of notch.

For the rectangular weir of the ordinary form the formula $D = 214 \sqrt{H^3}$ (where D is the discharge in cubic feet per minute for 1 foot width of weir, and H is the height of surface of water above sill in feet) is given in Beardmore's "Manual," and appears in Molesworth's "Pocket Book of Engineering Formulæ" and other published tables, and has long been in use.

The following is a simple formula, giving a very close approximation :—

$\sqrt{d} \ (d \times 5)$ = cubic feet per minute
Where d = the depth in inches flowing over weir for 1 foot wide.

This gives a slightly lower value than the preceding formula.

Hawkesley's abbreviated formula for a rectangular weir is as follows :—

$d \sqrt{d}$ = number of gallons per two seconds on 1 foot of weir.

This gives a slightly lower value than either of the preceding ones.

Where a gauge weir is fixed the channel should be enlarged, so as to form a large pool behind the weir, in order that the surface of the water may be still, and the velocity of the current reduced as much as possible, and the depth of water should be measured 3 or 4 feet behind the weir.

The gauge plate should not be more than $\frac{3}{4}$ to 1 inch thick, bevelled off to about $\frac{1}{4}$ inch thick at lip of sill, the bevel being on down-stream side of plate. For many of the experimental gaugings a very thin plate is used, in which the rectangular notch is cut, and it is stiffened by being attached to planking or otherwise , but the thicker plate is generally used, as being more suitable for a permanent gauge weir.

The formulæ quoted are applicable to such a weir ; but as the conditions of construction and arrangement of gauge weirs are liable to vary somewhat, it is impossible to obtain a formula that shall give exact results in all cases.

It is better to employ a formula likely to give results slightly below rather than in excess of the actual quantity passing over gauge weir.

The question of gauge weirs only occurs incidentally in this work, and it would be outside its scope to enlarge upon the subject.

There are many hydraulic works that treat of the matter Among others are Beardmore's well-known "Manual of Hydrology," Louis D. A. Jackson's and Box's Hydraulic Manuals, and Col. Moore's "Sanitary Engineering," already mentioned, besides Neville's "Tables and Formulæ," and numerous other published experiments and data.

Gauge Weir Discharge Recorder.—A very ingenious apparatus for recording the flow of water over gauge weirs is Hutchison's patent discharge recorder, shown by Fig. 101, manufactured by the Glenfield Company. There are other recorders for depth, but the special feature of this instrument is the recording of the actual discharge in gallons, or other measure of quantity. The discharge record is obtained from a cam, the curve of which is calculated from the formula for the discharge over the notch or rectangular weir under consideration. The cam, which is rigidly attached to a pulley actuated by the rise and fall of float, moves a pencil running in guides, which gives a true line of discharge upon diagram paper, wound upon a clockwork drum, making one complete revolution in a week.   There is a second pencil worked direct off float pulley, which gives the depth of

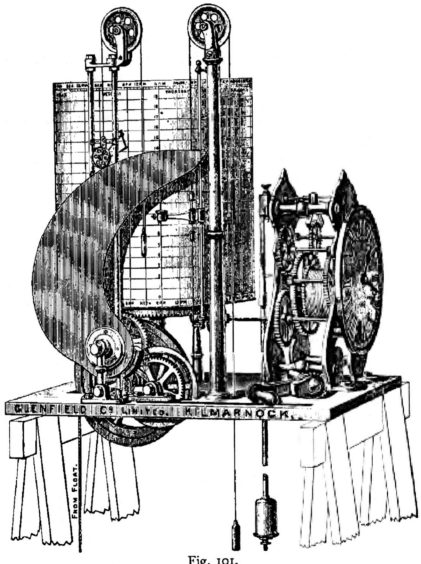

Fig. 101.

flow.   A blue line is marked upon diagram paper by the pencil for depth of flow, and a red line for discharge. The great advantage of the line of discharge is that the

actual quantity at any given instant can be read, and the
discharge for any period is got by taking the area of the
corresponding figure by a planimeter or otherwise. In
this way a great saving of trouble in getting out any
given discharge is effected.

Slide-Rule for the Regulation of Gauge Weirs.—
It will not be out of place here to refer to a slide-rule,
invented by the author, for the regulation of the water
over gauge weirs. It was found that when a given
quantity of water was being sent into a town supply
from more than one storage reservoir over separate
gauge weirs, if for local reasons a larger quantity had
to be sent from one reservoir, and the quantity from the
other reservoir correspondingly reduced to maintain the
same aggregate amount, it was necessary to have an
elaborate table of equivalents for the man in charge to
work from, which was always confusing and incomplete.
The slide-rule, where the conditions are as named, has
proved itself very satisfactory.

The lower portion of rule and slide are marked with
differential graduations for the varying depth of flow,
according to the formula for discharge, the graduations
upon lower portion of rule being set in opposite directions to those upon slide, and the quantities in gallons
are marked upon the top portion of rule opposite the
corresponding depths upon slide. Fig. 102 shows the
application of rule for the following example :—Supposing a quantity is being sent over one 3-foot weir equal
to a depth of flow of $9\frac{1}{2}$ inches, and a quantity equal
to a depth of flow of $6\frac{1}{4}$ inches over the second weir,
and it is required to increase the flow over the first
weir to 12 inches, and make an equivalent reduction
over the second weir, set the slide as shown in Fig. 102,
so that $6\frac{1}{4}$ inches upon same is opposite to $9\frac{1}{2}$ inches on

bottom of rule. You have then only to look for 12 inches upon the bottom of rule, opposite which will be found 2¼ inches upon slide, being the required depth of flow the second weir must be checked to, as an equivalent for the increase to 12 inches upon the first weir. In this way the equivalent for any alteration can be instantly found, on account of the depths markings being differentially graduated, according to the formula for discharge, so that they have constant quantity values from point to point on slide and rule.

With slide closed, it serves in lieu of a written table for depths of flow and quantities.

This slide-rule is also used where the supply is partly by pumping, and the remainder made up by flow over weirs from storage reservoirs. In this case there are markings upon the rule for the quantity values pumped by the engines; and in case of engines stopping or starting, the equivalent increase or decrease of flow of gravitation water over the weirs can be instantly obtained by the movement of the slide. The rule is also made in dial form with keyless motion, a pinion actuating a rack on an annular ring of the dial, which serves the same purpose as the slide in the rectangular rule.

Pressure-Recording Apparatus.—

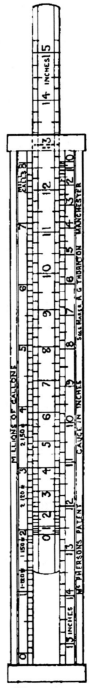

Fig. 102.

A pressure-recording apparatus is of great service upon
the trunk main supplying the water to a district, as it
records the varying pressures, and is a means of detecting
any abnormal head upon the main which might be
occasioned by a valve being partly closed, or through
any other cause; it also shows the fall in pressure due

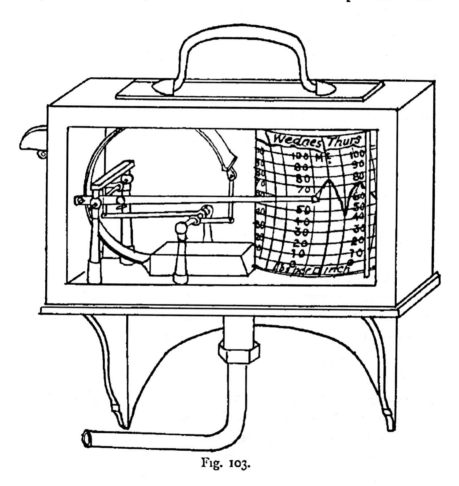

Fig. 103.

to a large leak or burst main, and enables the exact
time of any such occurrence to be fixed.

A very simple and efficient pressure-recording apparatus is shown by Fig. 103. It is by MM. Richard
Frères, of Paris, L. Casella being their London agent.

The well-known movement of a Bourdon tube, due to the pressure of the water, is magnified by the long arm of a lever, at the extremity of which a pencil is fixed, that indicates the pressure upon a diagram on a recording drum actuated by clockwork, the diagram being ruled horizontally for pressures, and vertically for measures of time, in the usual way. An electric alarm may be arranged in connection with this apparatus, which will make contact and ring an electric bell if the pressure becomes abnormal for either a rise or fall.

There are various other types of pressure-recording apparatus for water-pressure in mains, the clockwork, revolving drum or disc, and diagram being common to all; but the action may be obtained by means of a spring and piston arrangement, as in a Richardson steam-engine indicator, or by the pressure acting upon a corrugated diaphragm plate, or by a mercurial pressure-recorder

Water-Level Recorders. — Many very ingenious water-level recorders are produced by different makers, their object being to give a constant record of the change of level of the water in the service reservoirs or high-level tanks upon a system of distribution.

These instruments consist, broadly speaking, of two parts—the transmitter situated at the reservoir, the height of water in which has to be indicated ; and the recorder, which may be situated either at the central office under the control of the engineer-in-chief, or at the district pumping station, so that the engineman in charge there may regulate his pumping according to the height of the water in the tank. The transmitter and recorder may be any distance apart, a line wire connecting them.

The transmitting instrument transmits an electric

current for every 1 inch (or 2 or 3 inches if desired) rise or fall of water in reservoir.

There is a local battery in connection with the transmitting apparatus, and a float actuates a pulley for the rise and fall of the water. The pulley in one type of apparatus, by means of gearing, causes an insulated cam-wheel to make a complete revolution for every alteration in level of water of 1 inch. The cam-wheel engages a tumbler which throws the commutator over in opposite directions, according to the movement of the cam-wheel for a rise or fall, thereby making contact with one of the poles of the local battery, and, at the same time, a rubbing contact is set up between two springs by the movement of the cam-wheel, thus connecting electric current to line wire. The tumbler meanwhile in its descent completes the circuit. The current is thus transmitted through the line wire to the recorder.

The recorder has a clockwork movement, with a dial upon which the height of water in reservoir is registered, and a recorder with a recording diagram upon a drum. There is a local battery at the recorder, the current from the transmitter merely actuating the relay.

The current from the transmitter attracts at one pole of relay and repels at the other, according to its direction through the relay for a rise or fall, thus completing circuit with local battery. There are two electro-magnets at back of indicating dial, and according to the direction in which the current is passing, one or other of them attracts a soft iron core which moves a rack that engages toothed wheels which actuate the hand on indicating dial, and also the movement of the pencil which records the rise or fall upon diagram paper.

Before these recorders were in use the height of water in the reservoirs, if at any considerable distance from the pumping stations, had to be read upon a tell-tale by means of a telescope, or in foggy weather, or after dusk, it was a case of guess-work, or visiting the reservoirs.

In addition to the advantage of being able to tell at any time the height of water in the reservoirs, the recording diagram is of great service in order to ascertain the varying rate of consumption and maximum draught, and in many respects it is analogous to the waste water-meter diagram.

INDEX.

———◆———

Printed at THE DARIEN PRESS, *Edinburgh*

Standard Books

FOR

HYDRAULIC, WATER SUPPLY, AND SANITARY ENGINEERS

PUBLISHED OR SOLD BY

B. T. BATSFORD, 94 HIGH HOLBORN, LONDON.

Any of the works in this list will be forwarded post free in
the United Kingdom on receipt of the cash discount prices
quoted, except where postage is named as extra.

In the press. To be published shortly.

An entirely new and original series of Labour-saving Tables for
Hydraulic Engineers.

**TABLES FOR THE SOLUTION OF GANGUILLET AND
KUTTER'S FORMULA** FOR THE FLOW OF WATER IN OPEN
CHANNELS, PIPES, SEWERS, AND CONDUITS. In Two Parts. PART I.—
Arranged for 1,080 inclinations from 1 over 1, to 1 over 21,120, for 15
different values (n) PART II.—For all other values of (n). By Colonel
E. C. S. MOORE, R.E, M.S.I., Author of "Sanitary Engineering"
Containing upwards of 200 pages of original tables, specially computed,
together with a large folding diagram for finding the value of (c) graphically.
With explanatory text. Demy 8vo, cloth. (*Prospectus on application.*)

This work forms a COMPLETE SOLVER of the complicated formula of Messrs Ganguillet
and Kutter, now universally admitted to be the only reliable formula for hydraulic calculations. It has been compiled at considerable labour and great expense. No effort has been
spared to ensure accuracy Every result has been subjected to a special checking, and the
tables may therefore be taken as thoroughly reliable
As a work of reference for all engaged in Water Supply and Hydraulic Engineering it
cannot but prove of the greatest possible value and usefulness, and the immense saving of
time and labour by its use will commend it to every one who is called upon to make calculations involving Kutter's formula.

WATER-PIPE DISCHARGE DIAGRAMS, showing the Relation
between the Diameters, Gradients, and Discharges of Water-Pipes; together with other Diagrams, giving the Weights and Thicknesses of Pipes
for Various Pressures. Drawn and compiled by E B. TAYLOR, M.I.C.E.,
and G. M. TAYLOR, A.M.I.C E. 14 large diagrams, oblong folio (size
20 in. × 12½ in.), cloth. 10s. 6d.

"The book will save those devoted to waterworks engineering a good deal of time."—
The Engineer

THE WATER SUPPLY OF TOWNS AND THE CON-STRUCTION OF WATERWORKS.
A Practical Treatise for the Use of Engineers and Students of Engineering. By Prof. W. K. BURTON, A M I.C.E. Second Edition. Revised and extended. 318 pp., with 44 large folding plates and 258 diagrams in the text. Super-royal 8vo, buckram. 20s

I. Introductory II Different Qualities of Water   III. Quantity of Water to be Provided.   IV On Ascertaining whether a Proposed Source of Supply is Sufficient   V. On Estimating the Storage Capacity required to be Provided. VI. Classification of Waterworks   VII Impounding Reservoirs. VIII Earthwork Dams.   IX Masonry Dams   X The Purification of Water. XI Settling Reservoirs XII. Sand Filtration XIII Purification of Water by Action of Iron—Softening of Water by Action of Lime—Natural Filtration.   XIV. Service or Clean Water Reservoirs — Water Towers — Stand Pipes. XV. The Connection of Settling Reservoirs, Filter Beds, and Service Reservoirs. XVI Pumping Machinery. XVII Flow of Water in Conduits, Pipes, and Open Channels XVIII. Distribution Systems.   XIX Special Provisions for the Extinction of Fire XX. Pipes for Waterworks. XXI. Prevention of Waste of Water, etc.

THE WATER SUPPLY OF CITIES AND TOWNS.
By WILLIAM HUMBER, A M.Inst.C.E.   A comprehensive treatise.   Illustrated by 50 double plates and upwards of 250 illustrations of existing waterworks.   With 400 pp. of text.   Imp. 4to, strongly half bound in morocco.   £6. 6s. net., or a second-hand copy in good condition, £3. 15s. net. —

"The most systematic and valuable work upon water supply hitherto produced in English, or in any other language."—*Engineer.*

THE PRINCIPLES OF WATERWORKS ENGINEERING.
By J. H. T. TUDSBERY. M.I.C.E., and A. W. BRIGHTMORE.   Second Edition, revised, with an Appendix containing a series of 13 folding plates illustrating recently executed works.   Containing 440 pp. of text, with 120 diagrams.   Large 8vo, cloth.   20s.

CONTENTS.—I. Sources of Supply   II. The Measurement of Water. III. Collection. IV. Storage. V. Purification. VI. Conveyance. VII Distribution. VIII The Maintenance of Waterworks.

A TREATISE ON HYDRAULICS.
A Concise Manual for Engineers By Professor MANSFIELD MERRIMAN, C.E.   Illustrated by 104 diagrams, with numerous tables.   380 pages, large 8vo, cloth.   17s. net.

SUMMARY OF CONTENTS —I Introduction   II. Hydrostatics   III Theoretical Hydraulics.   IV. Flow through Orifices. V. Flow over Weirs VI. Flow through Tubes. VII Flow in Pipes. VIII. Flow in Conduits and Canals.   IX Flow in Rivers. X Measurements of Water Power. XI Dynamic Pressure of Flowing Water XII Hydraulic Motors, etc etc

PRACTICAL HYDRAULICS.
A Series of Rules and Tables for Engineers By THOMAS BOX   Tenth Edition. 8vo, cloth. 4s. (postage 2d.)

WELLS AND WELL-SINKING.
By JOHN GEO. SWINDELL, A.R.I.B.A., and C. R. BURNELL, C.E. Revised Edition. With a New Appendix on the Qualities of Water. Illustrated. 8vo, cloth. 2s.

B T. BATSFORD, 94 High Holborn, London, E.C.

WATER SUPPLY ENGINEERING: THE DESIGNING, CONSTRUCTION, AND MAINTENANCE OF WATER SUPPLY SYSTEMS, BOTH CITY AND IRRIGATION. By A. P. FOLWELL, C.E. 576 pp., with 19 full-page plates and 95 other illustrations. 8vo, cloth. **17s.** net.

LECTURES ON WATER SUPPLY, PROSPECTING FOR WATER, WELL-SINKING, AND BORING By JAMES MANSERGH, M.I.C E. 150 pp., with 23 large folding plates. Large 8vo, paper covers. **4s.**

THE WATER SUPPLY OF BARRACKS AND CANTONMENTS. By Major G. K. SCOTT-MONCRIEFF, R.E., A.M I.C.E. 343 pp., profusely illustrated by 60 large folding plates. 8vo, cloth. **10s. 6d.** net (postage 4d.).

WATERWORKS FOR THE SUPPLY OF CITIES AND TOWNS. With a description of the principal Geological Formations of England as influencing Supplies of Water By S. HUGHES, C.E., F.G.S. With 32 illustrations 8vo, cloth. **3s. 4d.** (postage 2d.).

WATER ENGINEERING. A Practical Treatise on the Measurement, Storage, Conveyance, and Utilisation of Water for the Supply of Towns, for Mill Power, and for other purposes. By C. SLAGG, A.M.Inst.C.E. Second Edition. Crown 8vo, cloth. **6s.** (postage 3d.).

"As a small practical treatise on the water supply of towns, and on some applications of water-power, the work is in many respects excellent."—*Engineering.*

RURAL WATER SUPPLY. A Practical Handbook on the Supply of Water and Construction of Waterworks for small Country Districts. By ALLAN GREENWELL, A.M.I.C.E., and W. T. CURRY, A.M.I.C.E., F G.S. With illustrations. Second Edition, revised. Crown 8vo, cloth. **4s.** (postage 2d.).

"A very useful book for those concerned in obtaining water for small districts, giving a great deal of practical information in a small compass."—*Builder.*

THE FILTRATION OF PUBLIC WATER SUPPLIES By ALLEN HAZEN. Third Edition, revised and enlarged, containing 330 pp., and numerous illustrations. 8vo, cloth. **12s. 6d.** net.

CONTENTS.—Continuous Filters and their Construction—Filtering Materials—Rate of Filtration and Loss of Head—Cleaning Filters—Theory and Efficiency of Filtration—Intermittent and other Methods of Filtration—Cost and Advantages of Filtration—Water and Disease—Reports and Statistics on European Water Supplies, &c

MICRO-ORGANISMS IN WATER, TOGETHER WITH AN ACCOUNT OF THE BACTERIOLOGICAL METHODS INVOLVED IN THEIR INVESTIGATION. Specially designed for the use of those connected with the sanitary aspect of Water Supply. By Professor PERCY FRANKLAND, F R.S. With 2 plates and numerous diagrams Large 8vo, cloth. **16s.** net.

B. T. BATSFORD, 94 High Holborn, London, E.C.

WATER SOFTENING AND PURIFICATION THE SOFTENING AND CIARIFICATION OF HARD AND DIRTY WATERS. By H. COLLET. 72 pp., illustrated. Crown 8vo, cloth. 4s. (postage 2d).

THE MICROSCOPY OF DRINKING WATER. By G. C WHIPPLE. 348 pp., with 19 full-page plates and other illustrations. 8vo, cloth 15s. net.

WATER ANALYSIS. A Practical Treatise on the examination of Potable Water. By J. A WANKLYN and E T. CHAPMAN Tenth Edition, containing 200 pp. of text. 8vo, cloth. 4s. (postage 2d.).

EXAMINATION OF WATER (CHEMICAL AND BACTERIOLOGICAL). By W. P. MASON. 146 pp., illustrated. 8vo, cloth. 5s 6d. net

WATER SUPPLY. Notes on the composition of Water and Sources of Supply, Purification, Modern Waterworks, Distribution, Water Rents and Charges, Domestic Supplies, Waste of Water, Water for Trade Purposes, &c. By JOSEPH PARRY, C E , Water Engineer, Liverpool. 8vo, cloth, 3s. 6d.

WATER SUPPLY CONSIDERED MAINLY FROM A CHEMICAL AND SANITARY STANDPOINT. By WM. RIPLEY NICHOLS, Professor at the Massachusetts Institute of Technology Fourth Edition Royal 8vo, cloth. 10s 6d net.

WATER AND ITS PURIFICATION. A Handbook for the Use of Local Anthorities, Sanitary Officers, and others interested in Water Supply. By S. RIDEAL, D.Sc With numerous illustrations and tables. 8vo, cloth. 6s. (postage 3d.).

PUMPS. THEIR PRINCIPLES AND CONSTRUCTION. A Series of Lectures delivered at the Regent Street Polytechnic, London. By J. WRIGHT CLARKE, Author of "Plumbing Practice." With 73 illustrations. 8vo, cloth. 2s (postage 2d.).

HYDRAULIC RAMS THEIR PRINCIPLES AND CONSTRUCTION. With results of some experiments carried out by the author. By J. WRIGHT CLARKE. 84 pp., with 36 illustrations. Crown 8vo, cloth. 1s. 8d.

PUMPING MACHINERY. A Practical Handbook relating to the Construction and Management of Steam and Power Pumping Machines. By W. M BARR. 450 pp., with 260 illustrations. Large 8vo, cloth. 20s.

THE CONSTRUCTION OF HORIZONTAL AND VERTICAL WATER-WHEELS. By W CULLEN. Illustrated by 11 plates 4to, cloth. 4s. (postage 2d.).

B. T BATSFORD, 94 High Holborn, London, E.C.

A MANUAL OF CIVIL ENGINEERING. By Professor W J. M. RANKINE. Twentieth Edition, thoroughly revised by W. J. MILLAR, C.E Containing 800 pages of letterpress, with upwards of 300 illustrations. Large thick 8vo, cloth. 12s 6d. (postage 4d.)

EARTHWORK SLIPS AND SUBSIDENCES UPON PUBLIC WORKS, THEIR CAUSES, PREVENTION, AND REPARATION. By J. NEWMAN, A. M.I.C.E. 230 pages of text. 8vo, cloth. 6s. (postage 3d.).

NOTES ON CONCRETE AND WORKS IN CONCRETE With reference especially to Public Works By J NEWMAN, A.M.I.C.E. Second Edition, revised and enlarged. Containing 200 pages of text. 8vo, cloth. 5s.

THE DESIGN AND CONSTRUCTION OF DAMS, INCLUDING MASONRY, EARTH, ROCK-FILL, AND TIMBER STRUCTURES, ALSO THE PRINCIPAL TYPES OF MOVABLE DAMS. By E. WEGMANAY, C.E. Illustrated by 97 full-page plates of examples of Dams actually carried out in various parts of the world. 250 pp. of text. 4to, cloth. 21s. net.

MASONRY DAMS FROM INCEPTION TO COMPLETION. Including numerous Formulæ, Forms of Specification and Tender, Pocket Diagram of Forces, &c. For the use of Civil and Mining Engineers. By C. F. COURTNEY, M.Inst C.E. 8vo, cloth. 7s.

RETAINING WALLS AND MASONRY DAMS. A Text-Book for Students and Engineers By Professor MANSFIELD MERRIMAN, C E 122 pp and 31 diagrams. Large 8vo, cloth. 8s. 6d. net.

A TREATISE ON MASONRY CONSTRUCTION By IRA O. BAKER, C.E. Fully illustrated by 10 folding plates and 125 diagrams. 556 pp., large 8vo, cloth. 21s net.

Part I. Materials. II. Preparing and using the Materials. III Foundations. IV. Masonry Structures—Dams, Retaining Walls, Bridge Piers, Abutments, Culverts, Arches, &c.

THE MUNICIPAL AND SANITARY ENGINEER'S HANDBOOK. By H. PERCY BOULNOIS, M.I.C.E. Third Edition, revised, with numerous illustrations. Demy 8vo, cloth. 12s.

HYDRAULIC MOTORS. TURBINES AND PRESSURE ENGINES. By G. R. BODMER, A.M.Inst.C.E. With 204 illustrations and numerous tables. Second Edition, thoroughly revised and enlarged. containing 550 pp. Thick 8vo, cloth. (14s.) 11s. 6d.

LABOUR-SAVING HYDRAULIC TABLES. By Colonel E. C. S. MOORE, R.E. See p. i.

B. T. BATSFORD, 94 High Holborn, London, E.C.

In the Press.   To be published shortly.

SECOND EDITION, THOROUGHLY REVISED AND GREATLY EXTENDED

Containing 800 pages of text, including 120 Tables, with 530 Illustrations and 100 large Folding Plates. Price (provisionally), 30s. net.

SANITARY ENGINEERING:

A PRACTICAL TREATISE

ON THE

COLLECTION, REMOVAL, AND FINAL DISPOSAL OF SEWAGE,

AND THE

DESIGN AND CONSTRUCTION OF WORKS OF DRAINAGE AND SEWERAGE;

With a Special Chapter on the Disposal and Destruction of House Refuse and Sewage Sludge;

AND

NUMEROUS HYDRAULIC TABLES, FORMULÆ, AND MEMORANDA, INCLUDING AN EXTENSIVE SERIES OF TABLES OF VELOCITY AND DISCHARGE OF PIPES AND SEWERS SPECIALLY COMPUTED FOR THIS WORK.

BY COLONEL E. C. S. MOORE, R.E., M.S.I.,

Author of " Sanitary Engineering Notes," " Tables for the Solution of Kutter's Formula," &c

"It is a great book, involving infinite labour on the part of the author, and can be recommended as undoubtedly the standard work on the subject.   . . The illustrations are most clearly drawn and reproduced, and the folding plates models of what such plates ought to be."—*The Builder.*

".   . The book is indeed a full and complete epitome of the latest practice in sanitary engineering, and no one interested in sanitation can afford to be without a copy of so comprehensive a manual.   . . As we have said before, this book is marvellously complete, the omissions few and trifling. AS A BOOK OF REFERENCE IT IS SIMPLY INDISPENSABLE."
—*The Public Health Engineer.*

"The subject is treated thoroughly and comprehensively, and the result is a work of reference which must find its way into every sanitary engineer's library. . . .   We may say in conclusion that we know of no single volume which contains such a mass of well-arranged information   It is encyclopædic, and should take its place as the standard book on the wide and important subject with which it deals."—*The Surveyor.*

B. T. BATSFORD, PUBLISHER, 94 HIGH HOLBORN, LONDON.

Lightning Source UK Ltd.
Milton Keynes UK
UKOW02f2246220614

233847UK00009B/83/P